LONGMAN LITERATURE

The Importance of Being Earnest

Oscar Wilde

Editor: Trevor Millum

LONGMAN

Longman Literature

Series editor: Roy Blatchford

Novels

Other titles in the Longman Literature series are listed on page 95.

Contents

The writer on writing

There is no such thing as a moral or immoral book. Books are well written or badly written. That is all.

Wilde himself said or wrote very little about writing. The quotation above – which so shocked the highly moral Victorian world – might suggest that the speaker was about to go on to describe what he meant by well or badly written. He did not. Wilde was the master of the short intriguing statement, or epigram, but rarely went on to develop such statements into anything more substantial.

For example, Wilde divided all books into three classes: books to be read, books to be re-read and books not to be read at all – especially all books that try to prove anything.

To tell people what to read is, as a rule, either useless or harmful; for, the appreciation of literature is a question of temperament not of teaching . . . but to tell people what not to read is a very different matter, and I venture to recommend it as a mission to the University Extension Scheme.

Pall Mall Gazette

Sometimes Wilde's characters spoke for him. 'The truth is rarely pure and never simple. Modern life would be very tedious if it were either, and modern literature a complete impossibility,' says Algernon in *The Importance of Being Earnest*. Later, Miss Prism remarks, 'The good ended happily, and the bad unhappily. That is what Fiction means.'

Whilst these views on literature, as on other subjects, are thought-provoking, they do not provide a very helpful insight into Wilde's writing or offer much advice to others on theirs! There is nothing particularly unusual about this. Writers are often unhelpful on the subject of writing, as are some painters on painting – and so on.

Perhaps instead we can turn to the literary experts for assistance. Though many of these critics concentrate on Wilde's life and the dramatic content of his plays rather than the nature of his writing, there are a number who have attempted to analyse his approach to the craft of writing itself.

Under Wilde's heading of 'books not to be read at all' would probably come most of the scores of books and articles which have been produced about his own writing, books and articles with titles such as *Romantic Pantomime in Wilde, Algernon's Appetite: Oscar Wilde's Hero as Restoration Dandy* and *Prunes and Miss Prism* . . .

Reading some of these critical studies of *The Importance of Being Earnest*, it is curious how many begin with statements such as:

> It is generally agreed that it is Oscar Wilde's masterpiece, but there is little agreement on why it should be thought so or on how it works as a play.
>
> David Parker, *Oscar Wilde's Great Farce*, 1974

> Almost everyone agrees that *The Importance of Being Earnest* is good fun, but few have tried to show that it is also a good play.
>
> Otto Reinert, *Satiric Strategy in The Importance of Being Earnest*, 1956

> Repeated revivals of *The Importance of Being Earnest* suggest that it has generally been found a very amusing and a very satisfying play. Accounts of why it is very amusing and very satisfying are harder to come by.
>
> Ian Gregor, *Comedy and Oscar Wilde*, 1966

If university professors and professional literary critics find it so hard to pin down what it is about Wilde's writing in `The Importance of Being Earnest` that makes it such a successful play, what chance does the student have?

However, one reviewer of another of his plays, *A Woman of No Importance*, praised him thus:

> . . . it is not his wit, then, and still less his knack of paradox twisting, that makes me claim for him a place apart among living English dramatists. It is the keenness of his intellect, the individuality of his point of view, the excellence of his verbal style and, above all, the genuinely dramatic quality of his inspirations.
>
> William Archer, 1893

If we are looking for some insight into his approach to writing, can we make a start here? The aspects which this review takes for granted, wit and paradox, are a good place to start.

It was accepted by all who knew Wilde or his works that he possessed great wit – a term difficult to define. If we describe someone as being witty we usually mean that he or she is capable of making amusing and intelligent remarks, often in quick response to something just said. For example, Algernon's response to Jack in Act 2:

> JACK   *Well, will you go if I change my clothes?*
>
> ALGERNON   *Yes, if you are not too long. I never saw anybody take so long to dress, and with such little result.*

page 37

What of the frequent mention of paradox? A paradox is a seemingly contradictory statement which on closer examination turns out to contain truth; for example, the old saying, 'Sometimes you have to be cruel to be kind', meaning that in a particular case stern treatment may benefit someone in the long run. In Wilde's case, some of the apparent paradoxes may – in a kind of double bluff – turn out to have no truth in them at all! For example, 'Divorces are made in Heaven' (page 3) or the following exchange in Act 1:

> ALGERNON   *All women become like their mothers. That is their tragedy. No man does. That's his.*
>
> JACK   *Is that clever?*
>
> ALGERNON   *It is perfectly phrased! and quite as true as any observation in civilised life should be.*

page 20

In other cases we can see the truth in the paradox, for example when Lady Bracknell comments on Lady Harbury's appearance: 'I hadn't been there since her poor husband's death. I never saw a woman so altered; she looks quite twenty years younger.'

What, though, does the reviewer William Archer mean by 'the excellence of his verbal style'? It is a description which does not get us very far – in fact, it is another way of saying that he wrote well! However, Wilde not only wrote well, he spoke well. Indeed, if Robert Ross (amongst others) is to be believed, he spoke more brilliantly than he wrote.

From the many accounts written at the time, it does seem clear that Wilde was a brilliant conversationalist. If that idea seems hard to grasp, perhaps it would help to think of him as the sort of guest whom every chat-show host would like to have on his or her programme. He would be entertaining by being witty, irreverent and appearing knowledgeable on a wide range of subjects. He would never be at a loss for something to say – usually something original and often something shocking – sometimes at the expense of other guests or the host. Given this talent, it is not surprising that Wilde's writing is at its best when it most closely resembles conversation – as it does in his plays, particularly his comedies – and especially in *The Importance of Being Earnest*. In conversation, whether his own or that of his characters, the wit, the paradox and the smart remark find their proper places.

sparkling dialogue and having a 'Gilbertian plot'. 'Gilbertian' means that it re-sembled the light operas of Gilbert and Sullivan, in which the plots were fre-quently absurd, melodramatic and amusing.

Wilde himself, when asked if he thought his play a success, said, 'It already is: the only question is whether the first night audience will be one too.' He is also quoted as remarking, 'The first act is ingenious, the second beautiful and the third abominably clever.' You can see that modesty was not one of Wilde's faults! In one of the paradoxes so typical of his conversation and his comedies, Wilde also made the much quoted remark that *The Importance of Being Earnest* was 'a trivial play for serious people'.

One of the few people who disliked it was the influential writer and critic Bernard Shaw, who thought it heartless:

I cannot say that I greatly cared for The Importance of Being Earnest. *It amused me, of course; but unless comedy touches me as well as amuses me, it leaves me with a sense of having wasted my evening.*

This reminds us that Shaw felt that drama had to both educate *and* entertain to be worthwhile.

What kind of humour?

   JACK *Is that clever?*
  ALGERNON *It is perfectly phrased!*

Wilde was a believer in art for art's sake. *The Importance of Being Earnest* seems to be an almost pure example of comedy for comedy's sake, wit for wit's sake . . . so do we need to find a reason, a moral, a point? What is the point of a witty remark in conversation? To be amusing, to encourage repartee, to decorate the exchange . . .

For the general theatre-goer it may well not matter whether the plot is Gilbertian or not, or whether it is farce or social comment. Audiences have found it funny and that seems to be sufficient. However, it might be worth asking in what way it is funny; what kind of humour does it employ?

The humour . . . lies in the adjectives, since they are merely the opposite of what is expected. Exchange them and the replies are commonplace. The trick was a useful one but Wilde used it too often.

CJL Price in *The Victorians*

An example would be Gwendolen saying: 'The old-fashioned respect for the young is fast dying out.'

But the humour of the play is not simply in its language. The plot is an amusing and complex combination of coincidental events building to an absurd climax. The play has been described as farcical, a description which implies extravagant humour of a very broad and improbable kind. It has also been called a 'comedy of manners' – a piece of writing poking fun at social conventions, vanities and hypocrisies. Jane Austen's novels would be examples of such writing, as would those of David Lodge and the plays of Alan Ayckbourn today.

There is also its sheer absurdity, the humour that comes from the ridiculous, for example Chasuble's reference to the Society for the Prevention of Discontent among the Upper Orders, or Cecily's engagement to Algernon before he knows of her existence. This style of humour, taken to extremes, has brought us *The Goon Show* and *Monty Python*.

The Importance of Being Earnest is a mixture of all these things, but it depends predominantly on the humour of witty repartee, the banter between the characters. And lively conversation depends largely (though not entirely) on Wilde's use of the paradox: the unexpected twisting of the expected into the unexpected.

In addition to all these aspects of its humour, *The Importance of Being Earnest* is also part of the tradition of melodrama – *Jane Eyre*, *Oliver Twist* and all those Victorian and Edwardian plays full of rediscovered brothers and orphaned babies.

His plays turn upon the disclosure of a shameful secret and 'a woman with a past' – well established Victorian devices. He is content to make use of the usual human furniture of the comedies of his day and of some of its more melodramatic conventions, but he is different from many of his contemporaries in being more interested in dialogue than character and in wit rather than situation.

CJL Price

Time and place

The Importance of Being Earnest is set in the late nineteenth century and the action takes place amongst people who are, by most standards, wealthy. They are upper class in their social status and take their position for granted. There is a good deal of snobbery and arrogance in their attitudes. This much would have been true of most of the upper classes of Victorian England and Ireland.

Wilde's central characters in *The Importance of Being Earnest* exhibit other qualities also. They do no work (can you imagine Jack or Algernon as soldiers or clergymen or members of parliament – some of the few careers open to the upper classes?) and are concerned only about their own pleasure and satisfaction. They are anxious to be fashionable and witty – but not intellectual or serious.

Social conventions – the 'correct' way of doing things – were very strong, as were the powers of parents and guardians over their children or wards. Marriage was looked at from a financial point of view as well as a romantic one. The world was a well-ordered place in which Queen Victoria ruled the British Empire and the British Empire dominated the world. The First World War and the Russian Revolution were only a few years away but as far as Lady Bracknell is concerned the most shocking event she can think of, the French Revolution, occurred a century before.

This is the social situation in which *The Importance of Being Earnest* takes place. A world where aunts are entertained to tea with cucumber sandwiches and weekends are spent at the country houses of one's friends or relations. It is a world where nothing is really taken seriously, except trivial things.

Just a trivial pursuit – or something more?

If, in *The Importance of Being Earnest*, nothing is really taken seriously except trivial things, can it be said that the play has nothing to contribute about any important issues? Is it just a trivial play about trivial people – perhaps for trivial people?

One commentator, CJL Price would say yes.

> No . . . acknowledgement of the real world is to be found in *The Importance of Being Earnest* and its reasoning is unclouded by sincerity. Pleasure alone matters; ideals are mere fancies.

Another critic, Eric Bentley, would disagree.

> Nothing is easier than to handle this play without noticing what it contains. It is so consistently farcical in tone, characterization and plot that very few care to root out any more serious content. The general conclusion has been that Wilde merely decorates a silly play with a flippant wit.

But Bentley goes on to claim that though the plot is absurd ('one of those Gilbertian absurdities of lost infants and recovered brothers') and the characters unbelievable, the dialogue contains a running comment on society, on themes of life which the plot itself never deal with: class, money, marriage, beauty, truth, morality and so on. Wilde's wit 'is not comic relief in a serious play but serious relief in an absurd play'.

In spite of all the issues mentioned by Bentley, it could well be argued that money is the main underlying concern of the play – and much of the play's wit is directed at the hypocrisy of a class which pretends that it is breeding or social status in which it is interested when what really matters is money.

A trivial comedy for serious people – or something more? Serious people have been taking *The Importance of Being Earnest* seriously for nearly a hundred years and audiences all over the world have been laughing at it for the same amount of time. Perhaps it is the fact that it is simply a very successful, very funny play that makes some people want to take it apart to see what makes it work. Meanwhile the audiences continue laughing . . .

■ Reading log

One of the easiest ways of keeping track of your reading is to keep a log book. This can be any exercise book or folder that you have to hand, but make sure you reserve it exclusively for reflecting on your reading, both at home and in school.

As you read the play, stop from time to time and think back over what you have read.

- Is there anything that puzzles you? Note down some questions that you might want to research, discuss with your friends or ask a teacher. Also note any quotations which strike you as important or memorable.

- Does your reading remind you of anything else you have read, heard or seen on TV or the cinema? Jot down what it is and where the similarities lie.

- Have you had any experiences similar to those narrated in the play? Do you find yourself identifying closely with one or more of the characters? Record this as accurately as you can.

- Do you find yourself really liking, or really loathing, any of the characters? What is it about them that makes you feel so strongly? Make notes that you can add to.

- Can you picture the locations and settings? Draw maps, plans, diagrams, drawings, in fact any doodle that helps you make sense of these things.

- Now and again try to predict what will happen next in the play. Use what you already know of the author, the genre (type of play) and the characters to help you do this. Later record how close you were and whether you were surprised at the outcome.

- Write down any feelings that you have about the play. Your reading log should help you to make sense of your own ideas alongside those of the author.

The Importance of Being Earnest

A trivial comedy for serious people

The cast

JOHN WORTHING, *JP*
ALGERNON MONCRIEFF
REVEREND CANON CHASUBLE, *DD*
MERRIMAN, *a butler*
LANE, *a manservant*
LADY BRACKNELL
HON. GWENDOLEN FAIRFAX
CECILY CARDEW
MISS PRISM, *a governess*

The scenes of the play

Act I *Algernon Moncrieff's flat in Half-Moon Street, in the West End of London.*
Act II *The garden at the Manor House, Woolton.*
Act III *Drawing-room at the Manor House, Woolton.*

Act One

Morning-room in Algernon's flat in Half-Moon Street. The room is luxuriously and artistically furnished. The sound of a piano is heard in the adjoining room.

Lane is arranging afternoon tea on the table, and after the music has ceased, Algernon enters.

ALGERNON Did you hear what I was playing, Lane?

LANE I didn't think it polite to listen, sir.

ALGERNON I'm sorry for that, for your sake. I don't play accurately – any one can play accurately – but I play with wonderful expression. As far as the piano is concerned, sentiment is my forte. I keep science for Life.

LANE Yes, sir.

ALGERNON And, speaking of the science of Life, have you got the cucumber sandwiches cut for Lady Bracknell?

LANE Yes, sir. (*Hands them on a salver.*)

ALGERNON (*inspects them, takes two, and sits down on the sofa*) Oh! ...by the way, Lane, I see from your book that on Thursday night, when Lord Shoreman and Mr Worthing were dining with me, eight bottles of champagne are entered as having been consumed.

LANE Yes, sir; eight bottles and a pint.

ALGERNON Why is it that at a bachelor's establishment the servants invariably drink the champagne? I ask merely for information.

LANE I attribute it to the superior quality of the wine, sir. I have often observed that in married households the champagne is rarely of a first-rate brand.

ALGERNON Good heavens! Is marriage so demoralising as that?

LANE I believe it *is* a very pleasant state, sir. I have had very little experience of it myself up to the present. I have only been married once. That was in consequence of a misunderstanding between myself and a young person.

ALGERNON (*languidly*) I don't know that I am much interested in your family life, Lane.

LANE No, sir; it is not a very interesting subject. I never think of it myself.

ALGERNON Very natural, I am sure. That will do, Lane, thank you.

LANE Thank you, sir.

Lane goes out.

ALGERNON Lane's views on marriage seem somewhat lax. Really, if the lower orders don't set us a good example, what on earth is the use of them? They seem, as a class, to have absolutely no sense of moral responsibility.

Enter Lane.

LANE Mr Ernest Worthing.

Enter Jack.

Lane goes out.

ALGERNON How are you, my dear Ernest? What brings you up to town?

JACK Oh, pleasure, pleasure! What else should bring one anywhere? Eating as usual, I see, Algy!

ALGERNON (*stiffly*) I believe it is customary in good society to take some slight refreshment at five o'clock. Where have you been since last Thursday?

JACK (*sitting down on the sofa*) In the country.

ALGERNON What on earth do you do there?

JACK (*pulling off his gloves*) When one is in town one amuses oneself. When one is in the country one amuses other people. It is excessively boring.

ALGERNON And who are the people you amuse?

JACK (*airily*) Oh, neighbours, neighbours.

ALGERNON Got nice neighbours in your part of Shropshire?

JACK Perfectly horrid! Never speak to one of them.

ALGERNON How immensely you must amuse them! (*Goes over and takes sandwich.*) By the way, Shropshire is your county, is it not?

2

JACK Eh? Shropshire? Yes, of course. Hallo! Why all these cups? Why cucumber sandwiches? Why such reckless extravagance in one so young? Who is coming to tea?

ALGERNON Oh! merely Aunt Augusta and Gwendolen.

JACK How perfectly delightful!

ALGERNON Yes, that is all very well; but I am afraid Aunt Augusta won't quite approve of your being here.

JACK May I ask why?

ALGERNON My dear fellow, the way you flirt with Gwendolen is perfectly disgraceful. It is almost as bad as the way Gwendolen flirts with you.

JACK I am in love with Gwendolen. I have come up to town expressly to propose to her.

ALGERNON I thought you had come up for pleasure?... I call that business.

JACK How utterly unromantic you are!

ALGERNON I really don't see anything romantic in proposing. It is very romantic to be in love. But there is nothing romantic about a definite proposal. Why, one may be accepted. One usually is, I believe. Then the excitement is all over. The very essence of romance is uncertainty. If ever I get married, I'll certainly try to forget the fact.

JACK I have no doubt about that, dear Algy. The Divorce Court was specially invented for people whose memories are so curiously constituted.

ALGERNON Oh! there is no use speculating on that subject. Divorces are made in Heaven –

Jack puts out his hand to take a sandwich. Algernon at once interferes.

Please don't touch the cucumber sandwiches. They are ordered specially for Aunt Augusta. (*Takes one and eats it.*)

JACK Well, you have been eating them all the time.

ALGERNON That is quite a different matter. She is my aunt. (*Takes plate from below.*) Have some bread and butter. The bread and butter is for Gwendolen. Gwendolen is devoted to bread and butter.

JACK (*advancing to table and helping himself*) And very good

3

bread and butter it is too.

ALGERNON Well, my dear fellow, you need not eat as if you were going to eat it all. You behave as if you were married to her already. You are not married to her already, and I don't think you ever will be.

JACK Why on earth do you say that?

ALGERNON Well, in the first place girls never marry the men they flirt with. Girls don't think it right.

JACK Oh, that is nonsense!

ALGERNON It isn't. It is a great truth. It accounts for the extraordinary number of bachelors that one sees all over the place. In the second place, I don't give my consent.

JACK Your consent!

ALGERNON My dear fellow, Gwendolen is my first cousin. And before I allow you to marry her, you will have to clear up the whole question of Cecily. (*Rings bell.*)

JACK Cecily! What on earth do you mean? What do you mean, Algy, by Cecily! I don't know any one of the name of Cecily.

Enter Lane.

ALGERNON Bring me that cigarette case Mr Worthing left in the smoking-room the last time he dined here.

LANE Yes, sir.

Lane goes out.

JACK Do you mean to say you have had my cigarette case all this time? I wish to goodness you had let me know. I have been writing frantic letters to Scotland Yard about it. I was very nearly offering a large reward.

ALGERNON Well, I wish you would offer one. I happen to be more than usually hard up.

JACK There is no good offering a large reward now that the thing is found.

Enter Lane with the cigarette case on a salver. Algernon takes it at once. Lane goes out.

ALGERNON I think that is rather mean of you, Ernest, I must say. (*Opens case and examines it.*) However, it makes no matter, for, now that I look at the inscription inside, I find that the thing isn't yours after all.

JACK Of course it's mine. (*Moving to him.*) You have seen me with it a hundred times, and you have no right whatsoever to read what is written inside. It is a very ungentlemanly thing to read a private cigarette case.

ALGERNON Oh! it is absurd to have a hard and fast rule about what one should read and what one shouldn't. More than half of modern culture depends on what one shouldn't read.

JACK I am quite aware of the fact, and I don't propose to discuss modern culture. It isn't the sort of thing one should talk of in private. I simply want my cigarette case back.

ALGERNON Yes; but this isn't your cigarette case. This cigarette case is a present from some one of the name of Cecily, and you said you didn't know any one of that name.

JACK Well, if you want to know, Cecily happens to be my aunt.

ALGERNON Your aunt!

JACK Yes. Charming old lady she is, too. Lives at Tunbridge Wells. Just give it back to me, Algy.

ALGERNON (*retreating to back of sofa*) But why does she call herself little Cecily if she is your aunt and lives at Tunbridge Wells? (*Reading.*) 'From little Cecily with her fondest love.'

JACK (*moving to sofa and kneeling upon it*) My dear fellow, what on earth is there in that? Some aunts are tall, some aunts are not tall. That is a matter that surely an aunt may be allowed to decide for herself. You seem to think that every aunt should be exactly like your aunt! That is absurd! For Heaven's sake give me back my cigarette case.

Follows Algernon round the room.

ALGERNON Yes. But why does your aunt call you her uncle? 'From little Cecily, with her fondest love to her dear Uncle Jack.' There is no objection, I admit, to an aunt being a small aunt, but why an aunt, no matter what her size may be, should call her own nephew her uncle, I can't quite make out. Besides, your name isn't Jack at all; it is Ernest.

JACK It isn't Ernest; it's Jack.

ALGERNON You have always told me it was Ernest. I have introduced you to every one as Ernest. You answer to the name of Ernest. You look as if your name was Ernest. You are the most earnest-looking person I ever saw in my life. It is perfectly absurd your saying that your name isn't Ernest. It's on your cards. Here is one of them. (*Taking it from case.*) 'Mr Ernest Worthing, B. 4, The Albany.' I'll keep this as a proof that your name is Ernest if ever you attempt to deny it to me, or to Gwendolen, or to any one else.

(*Puts the card in his pocket.*)

JACK Well, my name is Ernest in town and Jack in the country, and the cigarette case was given to me in the country.

ALGERNON Yes, but that does not account for the fact that your small Aunt Cecily, who lives at Tunbridge Wells, calls you her dear uncle. Come, old boy, you had much better have the thing out at once.

JACK My dear Algy, you talk exactly as if you were a dentist. It is very vulgar to talk like a dentist when one isn't a dentist. It produces a false impression.

ALGERNON Well, that is exactly what dentists always do. Now, go on! Tell me the whole thing. I may mention that I have always suspected you of being a confirmed and secret Bunburyist; and I am quite sure of it now.

JACK Bunburyist? What on earth do you mean by a Bunburyist?

ALGERNON I'll reveal to you the meaning of that incomparable expression as soon as you are kind enough to inform me why you are Ernest in town and Jack in the country.

JACK Well, produce my cigarette case first.

ALGERNON Here it is. (*Hands cigarette case.*) Now produce your explanation, and pray make it improbable.

Sits on sofa.

JACK My dear fellow, there is nothing improbable about my explanation at all. In fact it's perfectly ordinary. Old Mr Thomas Cardew, who adopted me when I was a little boy,

made me in his will guardian to his grand-daughter, Miss
Cecily Cardew. Cecily, who addresses me as her uncle from
motives of respect that you could not possibly appreciate,
lives at my place in the country under the charge of her
admirable governess, Miss Prism.

ALGERNON Where is that place in the country, by the way?

JACK That is nothing to you, dear boy. You are not going to
be invited.... I may tell you candidly that the place is not in
Shropshire.

ALGERNON I suspected that, my dear fellow! I have Bunburyed
all over Shropshire on two separate occasions. Now, go on.
Why are you Ernest in town and Jack in the country?

JACK My dear Algy, I don't know whether you will be able to
understand my real motives. You are hardly serious enough.
When one is placed in the position of guardian, one has to
adopt a very high moral tone on all subjects. It's one's duty
to do so. And as a high moral tone can hardly be said to
conduce very much to either one's health or one's happiness,
in order to get up to town I have always pretended to have a
younger brother of the name of Ernest, who lives in the
Albany, and gets into the most dreadful scrapes. That, my
dear Algy, is the whole truth pure and simple.

ALGERNON The truth is rarely pure and never simple. Modern
life would be very tedious if it were either, and modern
literature a complete impossibility!

JACK That wouldn't be at all a bad thing.

ALGERNON Literary criticism is not your forte, my dear fellow.
Don't try it. You should leave that to people who haven't
been at a University. They do it so well in the daily papers.
What you really are is a Bunburyist. I was quite right in
saying you were a Bunburyist. You are one of the most advanced Bunburyists I know.

JACK What on earth do you mean?

ALGERNON You have invented a very useful younger brother
called Ernest, in order that you may be able to come up to
town as often as you like. I have invented an invaluable

7

permanent invalid called Bunbury, in order that I may be able to go down into the country whenever I choose. Bunbury is perfectly invaluable. If it wasn't for Bunbury's extraordinary bad health, for instance, I wouldn't be able to dine with you at Willis's to-night, for I have been really engaged to Aunt Augusta for more than a week.

JACK I haven't asked you to dine with me anywhere to-night.

ALGERNON I know. You are absurdly careless about sending out invitations. It is very foolish of you. Nothing annoys people so much as not receiving invitations.

JACK You had much better dine with your Aunt Augusta.

ALGERNON I haven't the smallest intention of doing anything of the kind. To begin with, I dined there on Monday, and once a week is quite enough to dine with one's own relations. In the second place, whenever I do dine there I am always treated as a member of the family, and sent down with either no woman at all, or two. In the third place, I know perfectly well whom she will place me next to, to-night. She will place me next to Mary Farquhar, who always flirts with her own husband across the dinner-table. That is not very pleasant. Indeed, it is not even decent... and that sort of thing is enormously on the increase. The amount of women in London who flirt with their own husbands is perfectly scandalous. It looks so bad. It is simply washing one's clean linen in public. Besides, now that I know you to be a confirmed Bunburyist I naturally want to talk to you about Bunburying. I want to tell you the rules.

JACK I'm not a Bunburyist at all. If Gwendolen accepts me, I am going to kill my brother, indeed I think I'll kill him in any case. Cecily is a little too much interested in him. It is rather a bore. So I am going to get rid of Ernest. And I strongly advise you to do the same with Mr.... with your invalid friend who has the absurd name.

ALGERNON Nothing will induce me to part with Bunbury, and if you ever get married, which seems to me extremely problematic, you will be very glad to know Bunbury. A man who marries without knowing Bunbury has a very tedious time of it.

JACK That is nonsense. If I marry a charming girl like Gwendolen, and she is the only girl I ever saw in my life that I would marry, I certainly won't want to know Bunbury.

ALGERNON Then your wife will. You don't seem to realise, that in married life three is company and two is none.

JACK (*sententiously*) That, my dear young friend, is the theory that the corrupt French Drama has been propounding for the last fifty years.

ALGERNON Yes; and that the happy English home has proved in half the time.

JACK For heaven's sake, don't try to be cynical. It's perfectly easy to be cynical.

ALGERNON My dear fellow, it isn't easy to be anything nowadays. There's such a lot of beastly competition about.

The sound of an electric bell is heard.

Ah! that must be Aunt Augusta. Only relatives, or creditors, ever ring in that Wagnerian manner. Now, if I get her out of the way for ten minutes, so that you can have an opportunity for proposing to Gwendolen, may I dine with you tonight at Willis's?

JACK I suppose so, if you want to.

ALGERNON Yes, but you must be serious about it. I hate people who are not serious about meals. It is so shallow of them.

Enter Lane.

LANE Lady Bracknell and Miss Fairfax.

Algernon goes forward to meet them. Enter Lady Bracknell and Gwendolen.

LADY BRACKNELL Good afternoon, dear Algernon, I hope you are behaving very well.

ALGERNON I'm feeling very well, Aunt Augusta.

LADY BRACKNELL That's not quite the same thing. In fact the two things rarely go together.

Sees Jack and bows to him with icy coldness.

ALGERNON (*To Gwendolen*) Dear me, you are smart!

9

GWENDOLEN I am always smart! Am I not, Mr Worthing?

JACK You're quite perfect, Miss Fairfax.

GWENDOLEN Oh! I hope I am not that. It would leave no room for developments, and I intend to develop in many directions.

Gwendolen and Jack sit down together in the corner.

LADY BRACKNELL I'm sorry if we are a little late, Algernon, but I was obliged to call on dear Lady Harbury. I hadn't been there since her poor husband's death. I never saw a woman so altered; she looks quite twenty years younger. And now I'll have a cup of tea, and one of those nice cucumber sandwiches you promised me.

ALGERNON Certainly, Aunt Augusta.

Goes over to tea-table.

LADY BRACKNELL Won't you come and sit here, Gwendolen?

GWENDOLEN Thanks, mamma, I'm quite comfortable where I am.

ALGERNON (*picking up empty plate in horror*) Good heavens! Lane! Why are there no cucumber sandwiches? I ordered them specially.

LANE (*gravely*) There were no cucumbers in the market this morning, sir. I went down twice.

ALGERNON No cucumbers!

LANE No, sir. Not even for ready money.

ALGERNON That will do, Lane, thank you.

LANE Thank you, sir.

Goes out.

ALGERNON I am greatly distressed, Aunt Augusta, about there being no cucumbers, not even for ready money.

LADY BRACKNELL It really makes no matter, Algernon. I had some crumpets with Lady Harbury, who seems to me to be living entirely for pleasure now.

ALGERNON I hear her hair has turned quite gold from grief.

LADY BRACKNELL It certainly has changed its colour. From what cause I, of course, cannot say.

Algernon crosses and hands tea.

Thank you. I've quite a treat for you to-night, Algernon. I am going to send you down with Mary Farquhar. She is such a nice woman, and so attentive to her husband. It's delightful to watch them.

ALGERNON I am afraid, Aunt Augusta, I shall have to give up the pleasure of dining with you to-night after all.

LADY BRACKNELL (*frowning*) I hope not, Algernon. It would put my table completely out. Your uncle would have to dine upstairs. Fortunately he is accustomed to that.

ALGERNON It is a great bore, and, I need hardly say, a terrible disappointment to me, but the fact is I have just had a telegram to say that my poor friend Bunbury is very ill again. (*Exchanges glances with Jack.*) They seem to think I should be with him.

LADY BRACKNELL It is very strange. This Mr Bunbury seems to suffer from curiously bad health.

ALGERNON Yes; poor Bunbury is a dreadful invalid.

LADY BRACKNELL Well, I must say, Algernon, that I think it is high time that Mr Bunbury made up his mind whether he was going to live or die. This shilly-shallying with the question is absurd. Nor do I in any way approve of the modern sympathy with invalids. I consider it morbid. Illness of any kind is hardly a thing to be encouraged in others. Health is the primary duty of life. I am always telling that to your poor uncle, but he never seems to take much notice . . . as far as any improvement in his ailment goes. I should be much obliged if you would ask Mr Bunbury, from me, to be kind enough not to have a relapse on Saturday, for I rely on you to arrange my music for me. It is my last reception, and one wants something that will encourage conversation, particularly at the end of the season when every one has practically said whatever they had to say, which, in most cases, was probably not much.

ALGERNON I'll speak to Bunbury, Aunt Augusta, if he is still conscious, and I think I can promise you he'll be all right by Saturday. Of course the music is a great difficulty. You

11

see, if one plays good music, people don't listen, and if one plays bad music people don't talk. But I'll run over the programme I've drawn out, if you will kindly come into the next room for a moment.

LADY BRACKNELL Thank you, Algernon. It is very thoughtful of you. (*Rising, and following Algernon.*) I'm sure the programme will be delightful, after a few expurgations. French songs I cannot possibly allow. People always seem to think that they are improper, and either look shocked, which is vulgar, or laugh, which is worse. But German sounds a thoroughly respectable language, and indeed, I believe is so. Gwendolen, you will accompany me.

GWENDOLEN Certainly, mamma.

Lady Bracknell and Algernon go into the music-room; Gwendolen remains behind.

JACK Charming day it has been, Miss Fairfax.

GWENDOLEN Pray don't talk to me about the weather, Mr Worthing. Whenever people talk to me about the weather, I always feel quite certain that they mean something else. And that makes me so nervous.

JACK I do mean something else.

GWENDOLEN I thought so. In fact, I am never wrong.

JACK And I would like to be allowed to take advantage of Lady Bracknell's temporary absence...

GWENDOLEN I would certainly advise you to do so. Mamma has a way of coming back suddenly into a room that I have often had to speak to her about.

JACK (*nervously*) Miss Fairfax, ever since I met you I have admired you more than any girl... I have ever met since... I met you.

GWENDOLEN Yes, I am quite well aware of the fact. And I often wish that in public, at any rate, you had been more demonstrative. For me you have always had an irresistible fascination. Even before I met you I was far from indifferent to you.

Jack looks at her in amazement.

We live, as I hope you know, Mr Worthing, in an age of ideals. The fact is constantly mentioned in the more expensive monthly magazines, and has reached the provincial pulpits, I am told; and my ideal has always been to love some one of the name of Ernest. There is something in that name that inspires absolute confidence. The moment Algernon first mentioned to me that he had a friend called Ernest, I knew I was destined to love you.

JACK You really love me, Gwendolen?

GWENDOLEN Passionately!

JACK Darling! You don't know how happy you've made me.

GWENDOLEN My own Ernest!

JACK But you don't really mean to say that you couldn't love me if my name wasn't Ernest?

GWENDOLEN But your name is Ernest.

JACK Yes, I know it is. But supposing it was something else? Do you mean to say you couldn't love me then?

GWENDOLEN (*glibly*) Ah! that is clearly a metaphysical speculation, and like most metaphysical speculations has very little reference at all to the actual facts of real life, as we know them.

JACK Personally, darling, to speak quite candidly, I don't much care about the name of Ernest.... I don't think the name suits me at all.

GWENDOLEN It suits you perfectly. It is a divine name. It has music of its own. It produces vibrations.

JACK Well, really, Gwendolen, I must say that I think there are lots of other much nicer names. I think Jack, for instance, a charming name.

GWENDOLEN Jack?... No, there is very little music in the name Jack, if any at all, indeed. It does not thrill. It produces absolutely no vibrations.... I have known several Jacks, and they all, without exception, were more than usually plain. Besides, Jack is a notorious domesticity for John! And I pity any woman who is married to a man called John. She would probably never be allowed to know the entrancing pleasure

13

of a single moment's solitude. The only really safe name is Ernest.

JACK Gwendolen, I must get christened at once – I mean we must get married at once. There is no time to be lost.

GWENDOLEN Married, Mr Worthing?

JACK (*astounded*) Well... surely. You know that I love you, and you led me to believe, Miss Fairfax, that you were not absolutely indifferent to me.

GWENDOLEN I adore you. But you haven't proposed to me yet. Nothing has been said at all about marriage. The subject has not even been touched on.

JACK Well... may I propose to you now?

GWENDOLEN I think it would be an admirable opportunity. And to spare you any possible disappointment, Mr Worthing, I think it only fair to tell you quite frankly beforehand that I am fully determined to accept you.

JACK Gwendolen!

GWENDOLEN Yes, Mr Worthing, what have you got to say to me?

JACK You know what I have got to say to you.

GWENDOLEN Yes, but you don't say it.

JACK Gwendolen, will you marry me?

Goes on his knees.

GWENDOLEN Of course I will, darling. How long you have been about it! I am afraid you have had very little experience in how to propose.

JACK My own one, I have never loved any one in the world but you.

GWENDOLEN Yes, but men often propose for practice. I know my brother Gerald does. All my girl-friends tell me so. What wonderfully blue eyes you have, Ernest! They are quite, quite, blue. I hope you will always look at me just like that, especially when there are other people present.

Enter Lady Bracknell.

LADY BRACKNELL Mr Worthing! Rise, sir, from this semi-recumbent posture. It is most indecorous.

GWENDOLEN Mamma!

He tries to rise; she restrains him.

I must beg you to retire. This is no place for you. Besides, Mr Worthing has not quite finished yet.

LADY BRACKNELL Finished what, may I ask?

GWENDOLEN I am engaged to Mr Worthing, mamma.

They rise together.

LADY BRACKNELL Pardon me, you are not engaged to any one. When you do become engaged to some one, I, or your father, should his health permit him, will inform you of the fact. An engagement should come on a young girl as a surprise, pleasant or unpleasant, as the case may be. It is hardly a matter that she could be allowed to arrange for herself. ...And now I have a few questions to put to you, Mr Worthing. While I am making these inquiries, you, Gwendolen, will wait for me below in the carriage.

GWENDOLEN (*reproachfully*). Mamma!

LADY BRACKNELL In the carriage, Gwendolen!

Gwendolen goes to the door. She and Jack blow kisses to each other behind Lady Bracknell's back. Lady Bracknell looks vaguely about as if she could not understand what the noise was. Finally turns round.

Gwendolen, the carriage!

GWENDOLEN Yes, mamma.

Goes out, looking back at Jack.

LADY BRACKNELL (*sitting down*) You can take a seat, Mr Worthing.

Looks in her pocket for note-book and pencil.

JACK Thank you, Lady Bracknell, I prefer standing.

LADY BRACKNELL (*pencil and note-book in hand*) I feel bound to tell you that you are not down on my list of eligible young men, although I have the same list as the dear Duchess of Bolton has. We work together, in fact. However, I am quite ready to enter your name, should your answers be what a really affectionate mother requires. Do you smoke?

JACK Well, yes, I must admit I smoke.

LADY BRACKNELL I am glad to hear it. A man should always

15

have an occupation of some kind. There are far too many idle men in London as it is. How old are you?

JACK Twenty-nine.

LADY BRACKNELL A very good age to be married at. I have always been of opinion that a man who desires to get married should know either everything or nothing. Which do you know?

JACK (*after some hesitation*) I know nothing, Lady Bracknell.

LADY BRACKNELL I am pleased to hear it. I do not approve of anything that tampers with natural ignorance. Ignorance is like a delicate exotic fruit; touch it and the bloom is gone. The whole theory of modern education is radically unsound. Fortunately in England, at any rate, education produces no effect whatsoever. If it did, it would prove a serious danger to the upper classes, and probably lead to acts of violence in Grosvenor Square. What is your income?

JACK Between seven and eight thousand a year.

LADY BRACKNELL (*makes a note in her book*) In land, or in investments?

JACK In investments, chiefly.

LADY BRACKNELL That is satisfactory. What between the duties expected of one during one's lifetime, and the duties exacted from one after one's death, land has ceased to be either a profit or a pleasure. It gives one position, and prevents one from keeping it up. That's all that can be said about land.

JACK I have a country house with some land, of course, attached to it, about fifteen hundred acres, I believe; but I don't depend on that for my real income. In fact, as far as I can make out, the poachers are the only people who make anything out of it.

LADY BRACKNELL A country house! How many bedrooms? Well, that point can be cleared up afterwards. You have a town house, I hope? A girl with a simple, unspoiled nature, like Gwendolen, could hardly be expected to reside in the country.

JACK Well, I own a house in Belgrave Square, but it is let by the year to Lady Bloxham. Of course, I can get it back whenever I like, at six months' notice.

LADY BRACKNELL Lady Bloxham? I don't know her.

JACK Oh, she goes about very little. She is a lady considerably advanced in years.

LADY BRACKNELL Ah, nowadays that is no guarantee of respectability of character. What number in Belgrave Square?

JACK 149.

LADY BRACKNELL (*shaking her head*) The unfashionable side. I thought there was something. However, that could easily be altered.

JACK Do you mean the fashion, or the side?

LADY BRACKNELL (*sternly*) Both, if necessary, I presume. What are your politics?

JACK Well, I am afraid I really have none. I am a Liberal Unionist.

LADY BRACKNELL Oh, they count as Tories. They dine with us. Or come in the evening, at any rate. Now to minor matters. Are your parents living?

JACK I have lost both my parents.

LADY BRACKNELL To lose one parent, Mr Worthing, may be regarded as a misfortune; to lose both looks like carelessness. Who was your father? He was evidently a man of some wealth. Was he born in what the Radical papers call the purple of commerce, or did he rise from the ranks of the aristocracy?

JACK I am afraid I really don't know. The fact is, Lady Bracknell, I said I had lost my parents. It would be nearer the truth to say that my parents seem to have lost me.... I don't actually know who I am by birth. I was ... well, I was found.

LADY BRACKNELL Found!

JACK The late Mr Thomas Cardew, an old gentleman of a very charitable and kindly disposition, found me, and gave me the name of Worthing, because he happened to have a

17

first-class ticket for Worthing in his pocket at the time.
Worthing is a place in Sussex. It is a seaside resort.

LADY BRACKNELL Where did the charitable gentleman who
had a first-class ticket for this seaside resort find you?

JACK (*gravely*) In a hand-bag.

LADY BRACKNELL A hand-bag?

JACK (*very seriously*) Yes, Lady Bracknell. I was in a hand-bag
– a somewhat large, black leather hand-bag, with handles to
it – an ordinary hand-bag in fact.

LADY BRACKNELL In what locality did this Mr James, or Thomas, Cardew come across this ordinary hand-bag?

JACK In the cloakroom at Victoria Station. It was given to him
in mistake for his own.

LADY BRACKNELL The cloakroom at Victoria Station?

JACK Yes. The Brighton line.

LADY BRACKNELL The line is immaterial. Mr Worthing, I con-
fess I feel somewhat bewildered by what you have just told
me. To be born, or at any rate bred, in a hand-bag, whether
it had handles or not, seems to me to display a contempt for
the ordinary decencies of family life that reminds one of the
worst excesses of the French Revolution. And I presume you
know what that unfortunate movement led to? As for the
particular locality in which the hand-bag was found, a
cloakroom at a railway station might serve to conceal a
social indiscretion – has probably, indeed, been used for that
purpose before now – but it could hardly be regarded as an
assured basis for a recognised position in good society.

JACK May I ask you then what you would advise me to do? I
need hardly say I would do anything in the world to ensure
Gwendolen's happiness.

LADY BRACKNELL I would strongly advise you, Mr Worthing, to try and acquire some relations as soon as possible,
and to make a definite effort to produce at any rate one parent, of either sex, before the season is quite over.

JACK Well, I don't see how I could possibly manage to do
that. I can produce the hand-bag at any moment. It is in my

dressing-room at home. I really think that should satisfy you, Lady Bracknell.

LADY BRACKNELL Me, Sir! What has it to do with me? You can hardly imagine that I and Lord Bracknell would dream of allowing our only daughter – a girl brought up with the utmost care – to marry into a cloakroom, and form an alliance with a parcel? Good morning, Mr Worthing!

Lady Bracknell sweeps out in majestic indignation.

JACK Good morning!

Algernon, from the other room, strikes up the Wedding March. Jack looks perfectly furious, and goes to the door.

For goodness' sake don't play that ghastly tune, Algy! How idiotic you are!

The music stops and Algernon enters cheerily.

ALGERNON Didn't it go off all right, old boy? You don't mean to say Gwendolen refused you? I know it is a way she has. She is always refusing people. I think it is most ill-natured of her.

JACK Oh, Gwendolen is as right as a trivet. As far as she is concerned, we are engaged. Her mother is perfectly unbearable. Never met such a Gorgon. . . . I don't really know what a Gorgon is like, but I am quite sure that Lady Bracknell is one. In any case, she is a monster, without being a myth, which is rather unfair. . . . I beg your pardon, Algy, I suppose I shouldn't talk about your own aunt in that way before you.

ALGERNON My dear boy, I love hearing my relations abused. It is the only thing that makes me put up with them at all. Relations are simply a tedious pack of people, who haven't got the remotest knowledge of how to live, nor the smallest instinct about when to die.

JACK Oh, that is nonsense!

ALGERNON It isn't!

JACK Well, I won't argue about the matter. You always want to argue about things.

ALGERNON That is exactly what things were originally made for.

JACK Upon my word, if I thought that, I'd shoot myself.... (*A pause.*) You don't think there is any chance of Gwendolen becoming like her mother in about a hundred and fifty years, do you, Algy?

ALGERNON All women become like their mothers. That is their tragedy. No man does. That's his.

JACK Is that clever?

ALGERNON It is perfectly phrased! and quite as true as any observation in civilised life should be.

JACK I am sick to death of cleverness. Everybody is clever nowadays. You can't go anywhere without meeting clever people. The thing has become an absolute public nuisance. I wish to goodness we had a few fools left.

ALGERNON We have.

JACK I should extremely like to meet them. What do they talk about?

ALGERNON The fools? Oh! about the clever people, of course.

JACK What fools!

ALGERNON By the way, did you tell Gwendolen the truth about your being Ernest in town, and Jack in the country?

JACK (*in a very patronising manner*) My dear fellow, the truth isn't quite the sort of thing one tells to a nice, sweet, refined girl. What extraordinary ideas you have about the way to behave to a woman!

ALGERNON The only way to behave to a woman is to make love to her, if she is pretty, and to some one else, if she is plain.

JACK Oh, that is nonsense.

ALGERNON What about your brother? What about the profligate Ernest?

JACK Oh, before the end of the week I shall have got rid of him. I'll say he died in Paris of apoplexy. Lots of people die of apoplexy, quite suddenly, don't they?

ALGERNON Yes, but it's hereditary, my dear fellow. It's a sort of thing that runs in families. You had much better say a severe chill.

20

JACK You are sure a severe chill isn't hereditary, or anything of that kind?

ALGERNON Of course it isn't!

JACK Very well, then. My poor brother Ernest is carried off suddenly, in Paris, by a severe chill. That gets rid of him.

ALGERNON But I thought you said that... Miss Cardew was a little too much interested in your poor brother Ernest? Won't she feel his loss a good deal?

JACK Oh, that is all right. Cecily is not a silly romantic girl, I am glad to say. She has got a capital appetite, goes long walks, and pays no attention at all to her lessons.

ALGERNON I would rather like to see Cecily.

JACK I will take very good care you never do. She is excessively pretty, and she is only just eighteen.

ALGERNON Have you told Gwendolen yet that you have an excessively pretty ward who is only just eighteen?

JACK Oh! one doesn't blurt these things out to people. Cecily and Gwendolen are perfectly certain to be extremely great friends. I'll bet you anything you like that half an hour after they have met, they will be calling each other sister.

ALGERNON Women only do that when they have called each other a lot of other things first. Now, my dear boy, if we want to get a good table at Willis's, we really must go and dress. Do you know it is nearly seven?

JACK (irritably) Oh! it always is nearly seven.

ALGERNON Well, I'm hungry.

JACK I never knew you when you weren't....

ALGERNON What shall we do after dinner? Go to a theatre?

JACK Oh no! I loathe listening.

ALGERNON Well, let us go to the Club?

JACK Oh, no! I hate talking.

ALGERNON Well, we might trot round to the Empire at ten?

JACK Oh, no! I can't bear looking at things. It is so silly.

ALGERNON Well, what shall we do?

JACK Nothing!

ALGERNON It is awfully hard work doing nothing. However, I

don't mind hard work where there is no definite object of any kind.

Enter Lane.

LANE Miss Fairfax.

Enter Gwendolen. Lane goes out.

ALGERNON Gwendolen, upon my word!

GWENDOLEN Algy, kindly turn your back. I have something very particular to say to Mr Worthing.

ALGERNON Really, Gwendolen, I don't think I can allow this at all.

GWENDOLEN Algy, you always adopt a strictly immoral attitude towards life. You are not quite old enough to do that.

Algernon retires to the fireplace.

JACK My own darling!

GWENDOLEN Ernest, we may never be married. From the expression on mamma's face I fear we never shall. Few parents nowadays pay any regard to what their children say to them. The old-fashioned respect for the young is fast dying out. Whatever influence I ever had over mamma, I lost at the age of three. But although she may prevent us from becoming man and wife, and I may marry some one else, and marry often, nothing that she can possibly do can alter my eternal devotion to you.

JACK Dear Gwendolen!

GWENDOLEN The story of your romantic origin, as related to me by mamma, with unpleasing comments, has naturally stirred the deeper fibres of my nature. Your Christian name has an irresistible fascination. The simplicity of your character makes you exquisitely incomprehensible to me. Your town address at the Albany I have. What is your address in the country.

JACK The Manor House, Woolton, Hertfordshire.

Algernon, who has been carefully listening, smiles to himself, and writes the address on his shirt-cuff. Then picks up the Railway Guide.

GWENDOLEN There is a good postal service, I suppose? It may be necessary to do something desperate. That of course will require serious consideration. I will communicate with you daily.

JACK My own one!

GWENDOLEN How long do you remain in town?

JACK Till Monday.

GWENDOLEN Good! Algy, you may turn round now.

ALGERNON Thanks, I've turned round already.

GWENDOLEN You may also ring the bell.

JACK You will let me see you to your carriage, my own darling?

GWENDOLEN Certainly.

JACK (*to Lane, who now enters*) I will see Miss Fairfax out.

LANE Yes, sir.

Jack and Gwendolen go off. Lane presents several letters on a salver to Algernon. It is to be surmised that they are bills, as Algernon, after looking at the envelopes, tears them up.

ALGERNON A glass of sherry, Lane.

LANE Yes, Sir.

ALGERNON To-morrow, Lane, I'm going Bunburying.

LANE Yes, sir.

ALGERNON I shall probably not be back till Monday. You can put up my dress clothes, my smoking jacket, and all the Bunbury suits...

LANE Yes sir. (*Handing sherry.*)

ALGERNON I hope to-morrow will be a fine day, Lane.

LANE It never is, sir.

ALGERNON Lane, you're a perfect pessimist.

LANE I do my best to give satisfaction, sir.

Enter Jack. Lane goes off.

JACK There's a sensible, intellectual girl! The only girl I ever cared for in my life.

Algernon is laughing immoderately.

What on earth are you so amused at?

ALGERNON Oh, I'm a little anxious about poor Bunbury, that is all.

JACK If you don't take care, your friend Bunbury will get you into a serious scrape some day.

ALGERNON I love scrapes. They are the only things that are never serious.

JACK Oh, that's nonsense, Algy. You never talk anything but nonsense.

ALGERNON Nobody ever does.

Jack looks indignantly at him, and leaves the room. Algernon lights a cigarette, reads his shirt-cuff, and smiles.

Act Drop

Act Two

Garden at the Manor House. A flight of grey stone steps leads up to the house. The garden, an old-fashioned one, full of roses. Time of year, July. Basket chairs, and a table covered with books, are set under a large yew-tree.

Miss Prism discovered seated at the table. Cecily is at the back, watering flowers.

MISS PRISM (*calling*) Cecily, Cecily! Surely such a utilitarian occupation as the watering of flowers is rather Moulton's duty than yours? Especially at a moment when intellectual pleasures await you. Your German grammar is on the table. Pray open it at page fifteen. We will repeat yesterday's lesson.

CECILY (*coming over very slowly*) But I don't like German. It isn't at all a becoming language. I know perfectly well that I look quite plain after my German lesson.

MISS PRISM Child, you know how anxious your guardian is that you should improve yourself in every way. He laid particular stress on your German, as he was leaving for town yesterday. Indeed, he always lays stress on your German when he is leaving for town.

CECILY Dear Uncle Jack is so very serious! Sometimes he is so serious that I think he cannot be quite well.

MISS PRISM (*drawing herself up*) Your guardian enjoys the best of health, and his gravity of demeanour is especially to be commended in one so comparatively young as he is. I know no one who has a higher sense of duty and responsibility.

CECILY I suppose that is why he often looks a little bored when we three are together.

MISS PRISM Cecily! I am surprised at you. Mr Worthing has many troubles in his life. Idle merriment and triviality would be out of place in his conversation. You must remember his constant anxiety about that unfortunate young man his brother.

CECILY I wish Uncle Jack would allow that unfortunate young man, his brother, to come down here sometimes. We might have a good influence over him, Miss Prism. I am sure you certainly would. You know German, and geology, and things of that kind influence a man very much.

Cecily begins to write in her diary.

MISS PRISM (*shaking her head*) I do not think that even I could produce any effect on a character that according to his own brother's admission is irretrievably weak and vacillating. Indeed I am not sure that I would desire to reclaim him. I am not in favour of this modern mania for turning bad people into good people at a moment's notice. As a man sows so let him reap. You must put away your diary, Cecily. I really don't see why you should keep a diary at all.

CECILY I keep a diary in order to enter the wonderful secrets of my life. If I didn't write them down, I should probably forget all about them.

MISS PRISM Memory, my dear Cecily, is the diary that we all carry about with us.

CECILY Yes, but it usually chronicles the things that have never happened, and couldn't possibly have happened. I believe that Memory is responsible for nearly all the three-volume novels that Mudie sends us.

MISS PRISM Do not speak slightingly of the three-volume novel, Cecily. I wrote one myself in earlier days.

CECILY Did you really, Miss Prism? How wonderfully clever you are! I hope it did not end happily? I don't like novels that end happily. They depress me so much.

MISS PRISM The good ended happily, and the bad unhappily. That is what Fiction means.

CECILY I suppose so. But it seems very unfair. And was your novel ever published?

MISS PRISM Alas! no. The manuscript unfortunately was abandoned.

Cecily starts.

I use the word in the sense of lost or mislaid. To your work, child, these speculations are profitless.

CECILY (*smiling*) But I see dear Dr Chasuble coming up through the garden.

MISS PRISM (*rising and advancing*) Dr Chasuble! This is indeed a pleasure.

Enter Canon Chasuble.

CHASUBLE And how are we this morning? Miss Prism, you are, I trust, well?

CECILY Miss Prism has just been complaining of a slight headache. I think it would do her so much good to have a short stroll with you in the Park, Dr Chasuble.

MISS PRISM Cecily, I have not mentioned anything about a headache.

CECILY No, dear Miss Prism, I know that, but I felt instinctively that you had a headache. Indeed I was thinking about that, and not about my German lesson, when the Rector came in.

CHASUBLE I hope, Cecily, you are not inattentive.

CECILY Oh, I am afraid I am.

CHASUBLE That is strange. Were I fortunate enough to be Miss Prism's pupil, I would hang upon her lips.

Miss Prism glares.

I spoke metaphorically. – My metaphor was drawn from bees. Ahem! Mr Worthing, I suppose, has not returned from town yet?

MISS PRISM We do not expect him till Monday afternoon.

CHASUBLE Ah yes, he usually likes to spend his Sunday in London. He is not one of those whose sole aim is enjoyment, as, by all accounts, that unfortunate young man his brother seems to be. But I must not disturb Egeria and her pupil any longer.

MISS PRISM Egeria? My name is Laetitia, Doctor.

CHASUBLE (*bowing*) A classical allusion merely, drawn from the Pagan authors. I shall see you both no doubt at Evensong?

MISS PRISM I think, dear Doctor, I will have a stroll with you.
I find I have a headache after all, and a walk might do it
good.

CHASUBLE With pleasure, Miss Prism, with pleasure. We
might go as far as the schools and back.

MISS PRISM That would be delightful. Cecily, you will read
your Political Economy in my absence. The chapter on the
fall of the Rupee you may omit. It is somewhat too sensational. Even these metallic problems have their melodramatic side.

Goes down the garden with Dr Chasuble.

CECILY (*picks up books and throws them back on table*) Horrid Political Economy! Horrid Geography! Horrid, horrid German!

Enter Merriman with a card on a salver.

MERRIMAN Mr Ernest Worthing has just driven over from the
station. He has brought his luggage with him.

CECILY (*takes the card and reads it*) 'Mr Ernest Worthing, B. 4,
The Albany, W.' Uncle Jack's brother! Did you tell him Mr
Worthing was in town?

MERRIMAN Yes, Miss. He seemed very much disappointed. I
mentioned that you and Miss Prism were in the garden. He
said he was anxious to speak to you privately for a moment.

CECILY Ask Mr Ernest Worthing to come here. I suppose you
had better talk to the housekeeper about a room for him.

MERRIMAN Yes, Miss.

Merriman goes off.

CECILY I have never met any really wicked person before. I feel
rather frightened. I am so afraid he will look just like every
one else.

Enter Algernon, very gay and debonair.

He does!

ALGERNON (*raising his hat*) You are my little cousin Cecily, I'm
sure.

CECILY You are under some strange mistake. I am not little.
In fact, I believe I am more than usually tall for my age.

Algernon is rather taken aback.

But I am your cousin Cecily. You, I see from your card, are Uncle Jack's brother, my cousin Ernest, my wicked cousin Ernest.

ALGERNON Oh! I am not really wicked at all, cousin Cecily. You mustn't think that I am wicked.

CECILY If you are not, then you have certainly been deceiving us all in a very inexcusable manner. I hope you have not been leading a double life, pretending to be wicked and being really good all the time. That would be hypocrisy.

ALGERNON (*looks at her in amazement*) Oh! Of course I have been rather reckless.

CECILY I am glad to hear it.

ALGERNON In fact, now you mention the subject, I have been very bad in my own small way.

CECILY I don't think you should be so proud of that, though I am sure it must have been very pleasant.

ALGERNON It is much pleasanter being here with you.

CECILY I can't understand how you are here at all. Uncle Jack won't be back till Monday afternoon.

ALGERNON That is a great disappointment. I am obliged to go up by the first train on Monday morning. I have a business appointment that I am anxious . . . to miss?

CECILY Couldn't you miss it anywhere but in London?

ALGERNON No: the appointment is in London.

CECILY Well, I know, of course, how important it is not to keep a business engagement, if one wants to retain any sense of the beauty of life, but still I think you had better wait till Uncle Jack arrives. I know he wants to speak to you about your emigrating.

ALGERNON About my what?

CECILY Your emigrating. He has gone up to buy your outfit.

ALGERNON I certainly wouldn't let Jack buy my outfit. He has no taste in neckties at all.

CECILY I don't think you will require neckties. Uncle Jack is sending you to Australia.

ALGERNON Australia! I'd sooner die.

29

CECILY Well, he said at dinner on Wednesday night, that you would have to choose between this world, the next world, and Australia.

ALGERNON Oh, well! The accounts I have received of Australia and the next world, are not particularly encouraging. This world is good enough for me, cousin Cecily.

CECILY Yes, but are you good enough for it?

ALGERNON I'm afraid I'm not that. That is why I want you to reform me. You might make that your mission, if you don't mind, cousin Cecily.

CECILY I'm afraid I've no time, this afternoon.

ALGERNON Well, would you mind my reforming myself this afternoon?

CECILY It is rather Quixotic of you. But I think you should try.

ALGERNON I will. I feel better already.

CECILY You are looking a little worse.

ALGERNON That is because I am hungry.

CECILY How thoughtless of me. I should have remembered that when one is going to lead an entirely new life, one requires regular and wholesome meals. Won't you come in?

ALGERNON Thank you. Might I have a buttonhole first? I never have any appetite unless I have a buttonhole first.

CECILY A Maréchal Niel?

Picks up scissors.

ALGERNON No, I'd sooner have a pink rose.

CECILY Why?

Cuts a flower.

ALGERNON Because you are like a pink rose, cousin Cecily.

CECILY I don't think it can be right for you to talk to me like that. Miss Prism never says such things to me.

ALGERNON Then Miss Prism is a short-sighted old lady.

Cecily puts the rose in his buttonhole.

You are the prettiest girl I ever saw.

CECILY Miss Prism says that all good looks are a snare.

ALGERNON They are a snare that every sensible man would like to be caught in.

CECILY Oh, I don't think I would care to catch a sensible man. I shouldn't know what to talk to him about.

They pass into the house. Miss Prism and Dr Chasuble return.

MISS PRISM You are too much alone, dear Dr Chasuble. You should get married. A misanthrope I can understand – a womanthrope, never!

CHASUBLE (*with a scholar's shudder*) Believe me, I do not deserve so neologistic a phrase. The precept as well as the practice of the Primitive Church was distinctly against matrimony.

MISS PRISM (*sententiously*) That is obviously the reason why the Primitive Church has not lasted up to the present day. And you do not seem to realise, dear Doctor, that by persistently remaining single, a man converts himself into a permanent public temptation. Men should be more careful; this very celibacy leads weaker vessels astray.

CHASUBLE But is a man not equally attractive when married?

MISS PRISM No married man is ever attractive except to his wife.

CHASUBLE And often, I've been told, not even to her.

MISS PRISM That depends on the intellectual sympathies of the woman. Maturity can always be depended on. Ripeness can be trusted. Young women are green. (*Dr Chasuble starts.*) I spoke horticulturally. My metaphor was drawn from fruit. But where is Cecily?

CHASUBLE Perhaps she followed us to the schools.

Enter Jack slowly from the back of the garden. He is dressed in the deepest mourning, with crape hatband and black gloves.

MISS PRISM Mr Worthing!

CHASUBLE Mr Worthing?

MISS PRISM This is indeed a surprise. We did not look for you till Monday afternoon.

JACK (*shakes Miss Prism's hand in a tragic manner*) I have returned sooner than I expected. Dr Chasuble, I hope you are well?

31

CHASUBLE Dear Mr Worthing, I trust this garb of woe does not betoken some terrible calamity?

JACK My brother.

MISS PRISM More shameful debts and extravagance?

CHASUBLE Still leading his life of pleasure?

JACK (*shaking his head*) Dead!

CHASUBLE Your brother Ernest dead?

JACK Quite dead.

MISS PRISM What a lesson for him! I trust he will profit by it.

CHASUBLE Mr Worthing, I offer you my sincere condolence. You have at least the consolation of knowing that you were always the most generous and forgiving of brothers.

JACK Poor Ernest! He had many faults, but it is a sad, sad blow.

CHASUBLE Very sad indeed. Were you with him at the end?

JACK No. He died abroad; in Paris, in fact. I had a telegram last night from the manager of the Grand Hotel.

CHASUBLE Was the cause of death mentioned?

JACK A severe chill, it seems.

MISS PRISM As a man sows, so shall he reap.

CHASUBLE (*raising his hand*) Charity, dear Miss Prism, charity! None of us are perfect. I myself am peculiarly susceptible to draughts. Will the interment take place here?

JACK No. He seems to have expressed a desire to be buried in Paris.

CHASUBLE In Paris! (*Shakes his head.*) I fear that hardly points to any very serious state of mind at the last. You would no doubt wish me to make some slight allusion to this tragic domestic affliction next Sunday.

Jack presses his hand convulsively.

My sermon on the meaning of the manna in the wilderness can be adapted to almost any occasion, joyful, or, as in the present case, distressing. (*All sigh.*) I have preached it at harvest celebrations, christenings, confirmations, on days of humiliation and festal days. The last time I delivered it was in the Cathedral, as a charity sermon on behalf of the Society for the Prevention of Discontent among the Upper Orders. The Bishop, who was present, was much struck by some of the analogies I drew.

JACK Ah! that reminds me, you mentioned christenings I think, Dr Chasuble? I suppose you know how to christen all right?

Dr Chasuble looks astounded.

I mean, of course, you are continually christening, aren't you?

MISS PRISM It is, I regret to say, one of the Rector's most constant duties in this parish. I have often spoken to the poorer classes on the subject. But they don't seem to know what thrift is.

CHASUBLE But is there any particular infant in whom you are interested, Mr Worthing? Your brother was, I believe, unmarried, was he not?

JACK Oh yes.

MISS PRISM (*bitterly*) People who live entirely for pleasure usually are.

JACK But it is not for any child, dear Doctor. I am very fond of children. No! the fact is, I would like to be christened myself, this afternoon, if you have nothing better to do.

CHASUBLE But surely, Mr Worthing, you have been christened already?

JACK I don't remember anything about it.

CHASUBLE But have you any grave doubts on the subject?

JACK I certainly intend to have. Of course I don't know if the thing would bother you in any way, or if you think I am a little too old now.

CHASUBLE Not at all. The sprinkling, and, indeed, the immersion of adults is a perfectly canonical practice.

JACK Immersion!

CHASUBLE You need have no apprehensions. Sprinkling is all that is necessary, or indeed I think advisable. Our weather is so changeable. At what hour would you wish the ceremony performed?

JACK Oh, I might trot round about five if that would suit you.

33

CHASUBLE Perfectly, perfectly! In fact I have two similar cere-
monies to perform at that time. A case of twins that occurred recently in one of the outlying cottages on your own
estate. Poor Jenkins the carter, a most hard-working man.

JACK Oh! I don't see much fun in being christened along with
other babies. It would be childish. Would half-past five do?

CHASUBLE Admirably! Admirably! (*Takes out watch.*) And now,
dear Mr Worthing, I will not intrude any longer into a
house of sorrow. I would merely beg you not to be too much
bowed down by grief. What seem to us bitter trials are often
blessings in disguise.

MISS PRISM This seems to me a blessing of an extremely
obvious kind.

Enter Cecily from the house.

CECILY Uncle Jack! Oh, I am pleased to see you back. But
what horrid clothes you have got on! Do go and change
them.

MISS PRISM Cecily!

CHASUBLE My child! my child!

Cecily goes towards Jack; he kisses her brow in a melancholy manner.

CECILY What is the matter, Uncle Jack? Do look happy! You
look as if you had toothache, and I have got such a surprise
for you. Who do you think is in the dining-room? Your
brother!

JACK Who?

CECILY Your brother Ernest. He arrived about half an hour
ago.

JACK What nonsense! I haven't got a brother.

CECILY Oh, don't say that. However badly he may have behaved to you in the past he is still your brother. You
couldn't be so heartless as to disown him. I'll tell him to
come out. And you will shake hands with him, won't you,
Uncle Jack?

Runs back into the house.

CHASUBLE These are very joyful tidings.

MISS PRISM After we had all been resigned to his loss, his

sudden return seems to me peculiarly distressing.

JACK My brother is in the dining-room? I don't know what it all means. I think it is perfectly absurd.

Enter Algernon and Cecily hand in hand. They come slowly up to Jack.

JACK Good heavens!

Motions Algernon away.

ALGERNON Brother John, I have come down from town to tell you that I am very sorry for all the trouble I have given you, and that I intend to lead a better life in the future.

Jack glares at him and does not take his hand.

CECILY Uncle Jack, you are not going to refuse your own brother's hand?

JACK Nothing will induce me to take his hand. I think his coming down here disgraceful. He knows perfectly well why.

CECILY Uncle Jack, do be nice. There is some good in every one. Ernest has just been telling me about his poor invalid friend Mr Bunbury whom he goes to visit so often. And surely there must be much good in one who is kind to an invalid, and leaves the pleasures of London to sit by a bed of pain.

JACK Oh! he has been talking about Bunbury, has he?

CECILY Yes, he has told me all about poor Mr Bunbury, and his terrible state of health.

JACK Bunbury! Well, I won't have him talk to you about Bunbury or about anything else. It is enough to drive one perfectly frantic.

ALGERNON Of course I admit that the faults were all on my side. But I must say that I think that Brother John's coldness to me is peculiarly painful. I expected a more enthusiastic welcome, especially considering it is the first time I have come here.

CECILY Uncle Jack, if you don't shake hands with Ernest I will never forgive you.

JACK Never forgive me?

CECILY Never, never, never!

JACK Well, this is the last time I shall ever do it.

35

Shakes hands with Algernon and glares.

CHASUBLE It's pleasant, is it not, to see so perfect a reconciliation? I think we might leave the two brothers together.

MISS PRISM Cecily, you will come with us.

CECILY Certainly, Miss Prism. My little task of reconciliation is over.

CHASUBLE You have done a beautiful action to-day, dear child.

MISS PRISM We must not be premature in our judgments.

CECILY I feel very happy.

They all go off except Jack and Algernon.

JACK You young scoundrel, Algy, you must get out of this place as soon as possible. I don't allow any Bunburying here.

Enter Merriman.

MERRIMAN I have put Mr Ernest's things in the room next to yours, sir. I suppose that is all right?

JACK What?

MERRIMAN Mr Ernest's luggage, sir. I have unpacked it and put it in the room next to your own.

JACK His luggage?

MERRIMAN Yes, sir. Three portmanteaus, a dressing-case, two hat-boxes, and a large luncheon-basket.

ALGERNON I am afraid I can't stay more than a week this time.

JACK Merriman, order the dog-cart at once. Mr Ernest has been suddenly called back to town.

MERRIMAN Yes, sir.

Goes back into the house.

ALGERNON What a fearful liar you are, Jack. I have not been called back to town at all.

JACK Yes, you have.

ALGERNON I haven't heard any one call me.

JACK Your duty as a gentleman calls you back.

ALGERNON My duty as a gentleman has never interfered with my pleasures in the smallest degree.

JACK I can quite understand that.

ALGERNON Well, Cecily is a darling.

JACK You are not to talk of Miss Cardew like that. I don't like it.

ALGERNON Well, I don't like your clothes. You look perfectly ridiculous. in them. Why on earth don't you go up and change? It is perfectly childish to be in deep mourning for a man who is actually staying for a whole week with you in your house as a guest. I call it grotesque.

JACK You are certainly not staying with me for a whole week as a guest or anything else. You have got to leave . . . by the four-five train.

ALGERNON I certainly won't leave you so long as you are in mourning. It would be most unfriendly. If I were in mourning you would stay with me, I suppose. I should think it very unkind if you didn't.

JACK Well, will you go if I change my clothes?

ALGERNON Yes, if you are not too long. I never saw anybody take so long to dress, and with such little result.

JACK Well, at any rate, that is better than being always over-dressed as you are.

ALGERNON If I am occasionally a little over-dressed, I make up for it by being always immensely over-educated.

JACK Your vanity is ridiculous, your conduct an outrage, and your presence in my garden utterly absurd. However, you have got to catch the four-five, and I hope you will have a pleasant journey back to town. This Bunburying, as you call it, has not been a great success for you.

Goes into the house.

ALGERNON I think it has been a great success. I'm in love with Cecily, and that is everything.

Enter Cecily at the back of the garden. She picks up the can and begins to water the flowers.

But I must see her before I go, and make arrangements for another Bunbury. Ah, there she is.

CECILY Oh, I merely came back to water the roses. I thought you were with Uncle Jack.

ALGERNON He's gone to order the dog-cart for me.

CECILY Oh, is he going to take you for a nice drive?

ALGERNON He's going to send me away.

CECILY Then have we got to part?

ALGERNON I am afraid so. It's a very painful parting.

CECILY It is always painful to part from people whom one has known for a very brief space of time. The absence of old friends one can endure with equanimity. But even a momentary separation from any one to whom one has just been introduced is almost unbearable.

ALGERNON Thank you.

Enter Merriman.

MERRIMAN The dog-cart is at the door, sir. (*Algernon looks appealingly at Cecily.*)

CECILY It can wait, Merriman . . . for . . . five minutes.

MERRIMAN Yes, Miss.

Exit Merriman.

ALGERNON I hope, Cecily, I shall not offend you if I state quite frankly and openly that you seem to me to be in every way the visible personification of absolute perfection.

CECILY I think your frankness does you great credit, Ernest. If you will allow me, I will copy your remarks into my diary.

Goes over to table and begins writing in diary.

ALGERNON Do you really keep a diary? I'd give anything to look at it. May I?

CECILY Oh no. (*Puts her hand over it.*) You see, it is simply a very young girl's record of her own thoughts and impressions, and consequently meant for publication. When it appears in volume form I hope you will order a copy. But pray, Ernest, don't stop. I delight in taking down from dictation. I have reached 'absolute perfection'. You can go on. I am quite ready for more.

ALGERNON (*somewhat taken aback*) Ahem! Ahem!

CECILY Oh, don't cough, Ernest. When one is dictating one should speak fluently and not cough. Besides, I don't know how to spell a cough.

Writes as Algernon speaks.

ALGERNON (*speaking very rapidly*) Cecily, ever since I first looked upon your wonderful and incomparable beauty, I have dared to love you wildly, passionately, devotedly, hopelessly.

CECILY I don't think that you should tell me that you love me wildly, passionately, devotedly, hopelessly. Hopelessly doesn't seem to make much sense, does it?

ALGERNON Cecily!

Enter Merriman.

MERRIMAN The dog-cart is waiting, sir.

ALGERNON Tell it to come round next week, at the same hour.

MERRIMAN (*looks at Cecily, who makes no sign*) Yes, sir.

Merriman retires.

CECILY Uncle Jack would be very much annoyed if he knew you were staying on till next week, at the same hour.

ALGERNON Oh, I don't care about Jack. I don't care for anybody in the whole world but you. I love you, Cecily. You will marry me, won't you?

CECILY You silly boy! Of course. Why, we have been engaged for the last three months.

ALGERNON For the last three months?

CECILY Yes, it will be exactly three months on Thursday.

ALGERNON But how did we become engaged?

CECILY Well, ever since dear Uncle Jack first confessed to us that he had a younger brother who was very wicked and bad, you of course have formed the chief topic of conversation between myself and Miss Prism. And of course a man who is much talked about is always very attractive. One feels there must be something in him, after all. I daresay it was foolish of me, but I fell in love with you, Ernest.

ALGERNON Darling. And when was the engagement actually settled?

CECILY On the 14th of February last. Worn out by your entire ignorance of my existence, I determined to end the matter one way or the other, and after a long struggle with myself I

39

accepted you under this dear old tree here. The next day I bought this little ring in your name, and this is the little bangle with the true lover's knot I promised you always to wear.

ALGERNON Did I give you this? It's very pretty, isn't it?

CECILY Yes, you've wonderfully good taste, Ernest. It's the excuse I've always given for your leading such a bad life. And this is the box in which I keep all your dear letters.

Kneels at table, opens box, and produces letters tied up with blue ribbon.

ALGERNON My letters! But, my own sweet Cecily, I have never written you any letters.

CECILY You need hardly remind me of that, Ernest. I remember only too well that I was forced to write your letters for you. I wrote always three times a week, and sometimes oftener.

ALGERNON Oh, do let me read them, Cecily?

CECILY Oh, I couldn't possibly. They would make you far too conceited. (*Replaces box.*) The three you wrote me after I had broken off the engagement are so beautiful, and so badly spelled, that even now I can hardly read them without crying a little.

ALGERNON But was our engagement ever broken off?

CECILY Of course it was. On the 22nd of last March. You can see the entry if you like. (*Shows diary.*) 'To-day I broke off my engagement with Ernest. I feel it is better to do so. The weather still continues charming.'

ALGERNON But why on earth did you break it off? What had I done? I had done nothing at all. Cecily, I am very much hurt indeed to hear you broke it off. Particularly when the weather was so charming.

CECILY It would hardly have been a really serious engagement if it hadn't been broken off at least once. But I forgave you before the week was out.

ALGERNON (*crossing to her, and kneeling*) What a perfect angel you are, Cecily.

CECILY You dear romantic boy.

He kisses her, she puts her fingers through his hair.

I hope your hair curls naturally, does it?

ALGERNON Yes, darling, with a little help from others.

CECILY I am so glad.

ALGERNON You'll never break off our engagement again Cecily?

CECILY I don't think I could break it off now that I have actually met you. Besides, of course, there is the question of your name.

ALGERNON Yes, of course. (*Nervously.*)

CECILY You must not laugh at me, darling, but it had always been a girlish dream of mine to love some one whose name was Ernest.

Algernon rises, Cecily also.

There is something in that name that seems to inspire absolute confidence. I pity any poor married woman whose husband is not called Ernest.

ALGERNON But, my dear child, do you mean to say you could not love me if I had some other name?

CECILY But what name?

ALGERNON Oh, any name you like – Algernon – for instance . . .

CECILY But I don't like the name of Algernon.

ALGERNON Well, my own dear, sweet, loving little darling, I really can't see why you should object to the name of Algernon. It is not at all a bad name. In fact, it is rather an aristocratic name. Half of the chaps who get into the Bankruptcy Court are called Algernon. But seriously, Cecily . . . (*Moving to her*) . . . if my name was Algy, couldn't you love me?

CECILY (*rising*) I might respect you, Ernest, I might admire your character, but I fear that I should not be able to give you my undivided attention.

ALGERNON Ahem! Cecily! (*Picking up hat.*) Your Rector here is, I suppose, thoroughly experienced in the practice of all the rites and ceremonials of the Church?

CECILY Oh, yes. Dr Chasuble is a most learned man. He has

never written a single book, so you can imagine how much he knows.

ALGERNON I must see him at once on a most important chris-tening – I mean on most important business.

CECILY Oh!

ALGERNON I shan't be away more than half an hour.

CECILY Considering that we have been engaged since Febru-ary the 14th, and that I only met you to-day for the first time, I think it is rather hard that you should leave me for so long a period as half an hour. Couldn't you make it twenty minutes?

ALGERNON I'll be back in no time.

Kisses her and rushes down the garden.

CECILY What an impetuous boy he is! I like his hair so much. I must enter his proposal in my diary.

Enter Merriman.

MERRIMAN A Miss Fairfax has just called to see Mr Worthing. On very important business, Miss Fairfax states.

CECILY Isn't Mr Worthing in his library?

MERRIMAN Mr Worthing went over in the direction of the Rec-tory some time ago.

CECILY Pray ask the lady to come out here; Mr Worthing is sure to be back soon. And you can bring tea.

MERRIMAN Yes, Miss.

Goes out.

CECILY Miss Fairfax! I suppose one of the many good elderly women who are associated with Uncle Jack in some of his philanthropic work in London. I don't quite like women who are interested in philanthropic work. I think it is so forward of them.

Enter Merriman.

MERRIMAN Miss Fairfax.

Enter Gwendolen. Exit Merriman.

CECILY (*advancing to meet her*) Pray let me introduce myself to you. My name is Cecily Cardew.

GWENDOLEN Cecily Cardew? (*Moving to her and shaking hands.*)

What a very sweet name! Something tells me that we are going to be great friends. I like you already more than I can say. My first impressions of people are never wrong.

CECILY How nice of you to like me so much after we have known each other such a comparatively short time. Pray sit down.

GWENDOLEN (*still standing up*) I may call you Cecily, may I not?

CECILY With pleasure!

GWENDOLEN And you will always call me Gwendolen won't you?

CECILY If you wish.

GWENDOLEN Then that is all quite settled, is it not?

CECILY I hope so.

A pause. They both sit down together.

GWENDOLEN Perhaps this might be a favourable opportunity for my mentioning who I am. My father is Lord Bracknell. You have never heard of papa, I suppose?

CECILY I don't think so.

GWENDOLEN Outside the family circle, papa, I am glad to say, is entirely unknown. I think that is quite as it should be. The home seems to me to be the proper sphere for the man. And certainly once a man begins to neglect his domestic duties he becomes painfully effeminate, does he not? And I don't like that. It makes men so very attractive. Cecily, mamma, whose views on education are remarkably strict, has brought me up to be extremely short-sighted; it is part of her system; so do you mind my looking at you through my glasses?

CECILY Oh! not at all, Gwendolen. I am very fond of being looked at.

GWENDOLEN (*after examining Cecily carefully through a lorgnette*) You are here on a short visit, I suppose.

CECILY Oh no! I live here.

GWENDOLEN (*severely*) Really? Your mother, no doubt, or some female relative of advanced years, resides here also?

CECILY Oh no! I have no mother, nor, in fact, any relations.

GWENDOLEN Indeed?

CECILY My dear guardian, with the assistance of Miss Prism, has the arduous task of looking after me.

GWENDOLEN Your guardian?

CECILY Yes, I am Mr Worthing's ward.

GWENDOLEN Oh! It is strange he never mentioned to me that he had a ward. How secretive of him! He grows more interesting hourly. I am not sure, however, that the news inspires me with feelings of unmixed delight. (*Rising and going to her.*) I am very fond of you, Cecily; I have liked you ever since I met you! But I am bound to state that now that I know that you are Mr Worthing's ward, I cannot help expressing a wish you were – well, just a little older than you seem to be – and not quite so very alluring in appearance. In fact, if I may speak candidly –

CECILY Pray do! I think that whenever one has anything unpleasant to say, one should always be quite candid.

GWENDOLEN Well, to speak with perfect candour, Cecily, I wish that you were fully forty-two, and more than usually plain for your age. Ernest has a strong upright nature. He is the very soul of truth and honour. Disloyalty would be as impossible to him as deception. But even men of the noblest possible moral character are extremely susceptible to the influence of the physical charms of others. Modern, no less than Ancient History, supplies us with many most painful examples of what I refer to. If it were not so, indeed, History would be quite unreadable.

CECILY I beg your pardon, Gwendolen, did you say Ernest?

GWENDOLEN Yes.

CECILY Oh, but it is not Mr Ernest Worthing who is my guardian. It is his brother – his elder brother.

GWENDOLEN (*sitting down again*) Ernest never mentioned to me that he had a brother.

CECILY I am sorry to say they have not been on good terms for a long time.

GWENDOLEN Ah! that accounts for it. And now that I think of it I have never heard any man mention his brother. The subject seems distasteful to most men. Cecily, you have lifted a load from my mind. I was growing almost anxious. It would have been terrible if any cloud had come across a friendship like ours, would it not? Of course you are quite, quite sure that it is not Mr Ernest Worthing who is your guardian?

CECILY Quite sure. (*A pause.*) In fact, I am going to be his.

GWENDOLEN (*inquiringly.*) I beg your pardon?

CECILY (*rather shy and confidingly*) Dearest Gwendolen, there is no reason why I should make a secret of it to you. Our little country newspaper is sure to chronicle the fact next week. Mr Ernest Worthing and I are engaged to be married.

GWENDOLEN (*quite politely, rising*) My darling Cecily, I think there must be some slight error. Mr Ernest Worthing is engaged to me. The announcement will appear in the *Morning Post* on Saturday at the latest.

CECILY (*very politely, rising*) I am afraid you must be under some misconception. Ernest proposed to me exactly ten minutes ago.

Shows diary.

GWENDOLEN (*examines diary through her lorgnette carefully.*) It is certainly very curious, for he asked me to be his wife yesterday afternoon at 5.30. If you would care to verify the incident, pray do so. (*Produces diary of her own.*) I never travel without my diary. One should always have something sensational to read in the train. I am so sorry, dear Cecily, if it is any disappointment to you, but I am afraid I have the prior claim.

CECILY It would distress me more than I can tell you, dear Gwendolen, if it caused you any mental or physical anguish, but I feel bound to point out that since Ernest proposed to you he clearly has changed his mind.

GWENDOLEN (*meditatively*) If the poor fellow has been entrapped into any foolish promise I shall consider it my duty to

45

rescue him at once, and with a firm hand.

CECILY (*thoughtfully and sadly*) Whatever unfortunate entanglement my dear boy may have got into, I will never reproach him with it after we are married.

GWENDOLEN Do you allude to me, Miss Cardew, as an entanglement? You are presumptuous. On an occasion of this kind it becomes more than a moral duty to speak one's mind. It becomes a pleasure.

CECILY Do you suggest, Miss Fairfax, that I entrapped Ernest into an engagement? How dare you? This is no time for wearing the shallow mask of manner. When I see a spade I call it a spade.

GWENDOLEN (*satirically*) I am glad to say that I have never seen a spade. It is obvious that our social spheres have been widely different.

Enter Merriman, followed by the footman. He carries a salver, table cloth, and plate stand. Cecily is about to retort. The presence of the servants exercises a restraining influence, under which both girls chafe.

MERRIMAN Shall I lay tea here as usual, Miss?

CECILY (*sternly, in a calm voice*) Yes, as usual.

Merriman begins to clear table and lay cloth. A long pause. Cecily and Gwendolen glare at each other.

GWENDOLEN Are there many interesting walks in the vicinity, Miss Cardew?

CECILY Oh! yes! a great many. From the top of one of the hills quite close one can see five counties.

GWENDOLEN Five counties! I don't think I should like that; I hate crowds.

CECILY (*sweetly*) I suppose that is why you live in town?

Gwendolen bites her lip, and beats her foot nervously with her parasol.

GWENDOLEN (*looking round*) Quite a well-kept garden this is, Miss Cardew.

CECILY So glad you like it, Miss Fairfax.

GWENDOLEN I had no idea there were any flowers in the country.

CECILY Oh, flowers are as common here, Miss Fairfax, as

people are in London.

GWENDOLEN Personally I cannot understand how anybody manages to exist in the country, if anybody who is anybody does. The country always bores me to death.

CECILY Ah! This is what the newspapers call agricultural depression, is it not? I believe the aristocracy are suffering very much from it just at present. It is almost an epidemic amongst them, I have been told. May I offer you some tea, Miss Fairfax?

GWENDOLEN (*with elaborate politeness*) Thank you. (*Aside.*) Detestable girl. But I require tea!

CECILY (*sweetly*) Sugar?

GWENDOLEN (*superciliously*) No, thank you. Sugar is not fashionable any more.

Cecily looks angrily at her, takes up the tongs and puts four lumps of sugar into the cup.

CECILY (*severely*) Cake or bread and butter?

GWENDOLEN (*in a bored manner*) Bread and butter, please. Cake is rarely seen at the best houses nowadays.

CECILY (*cuts a very large slice of cake, and puts it on the tray*) Hand that to Miss Fairfax.

Merriman does so, and goes out with footman. Gwendolen drinks the tea and makes a grimace. Puts down cup at once, reaches out her hand to the bread and butter, looks at it, and finds it is cake. Rises in indignation.

GWENDOLEN You have filled my tea with lumps of sugar, and though I asked most distinctly for bread and butter, you have given me cake. I am known for the gentleness of my disposition, and the extraordinary sweetness of my nature, but I warn you, Miss Cardew, you may go too far.

CECILY (*rising*) To save my poor, innocent, trusting boy from the machinations of any other girl there are no lengths to which I would not go.

GWENDOLEN From the moment I saw you I distrusted you. I felt that you were false and deceitful. I am never deceived in such matters. My first impressions of people are invariably right.

CECILY It seems to me, Miss Fairfax, that I am trespassing on your valuable time. No doubt you have many other calls of a similar character to make in the neighbourhood.

Enter Jack.

GWENDOLEN (*catching sight of him*) Ernest! My own Ernest!

JACK Gwendolen! Darling!

Offers to kiss her.

GWENDOLEN (*drawing back*) A moment! May I ask if you are engaged to be married to this young lady?

Points to Cecily.

JACK (*laughing*) To dear little Cecily! Of course not! What could have put such an idea into your pretty little head?

GWENDOLEN Thank you. You may!

Offers her cheek.

CECILY (*very sweetly*) I knew there must be some misunderstanding, Miss Fairfax. The gentleman whose arm is at present round your waist is my guardian, Mr John Worthing.

GWENDOLEN I beg your pardon?

CECILY This is Uncle Jack.

GWENDOLEN (*receding*) Jack! Oh!

Enter Algernon.

CECILY Here is Ernest.

ALGERNON (*goes straight over to Cecily without noticing any one else*) My own love!

Offers to kiss her.

CECILY (*drawing back*) A moment, Ernest! May I ask you – are you engaged to be married to this young lady?

ALGERNON (*looking round*) To what young lady? Good heavens! Gwendolen!

CECILY Yes! to good heavens, Gwendolen, I mean to Gwendolen.

ALGERNON (*laughing*) Of course not! What could have put such an idea into your pretty little head?

CECILY Thank you. (*Presenting her cheek to be kissed.*) You may.

Algernon kisses her.

GWENDOLEN I felt there was some slight error, Miss Cardew. The gentleman who is now embracing you is my cousin, Mr. Algernon Moncrieff.

CECILY (*breaking away from Algernon*) Algernon Moncrieff! Oh!
The two girls move towards each other and put their arms round each other's waists as if for protection.

CECILY Are you called Algernon?

ALGERNON I cannot deny it.

CECILY Oh!

GWENDOLEN Is your name really John?

JACK (*standing rather proudly*) I could deny it if I liked. I could deny anything if I liked. But my name certainly is John. It has been John for years.

CECILY (*to Gwendolen*) A gross deception has been practised on both of us.

GWENDOLEN My poor wounded Cecily!

CECILY My sweet wronged Gwendolen!

GWENDOLEN (*slowly and seriously*) You will call me sister, will you not?
They embrace. Jack and Algernon groan and walk up and down.

CECILY (*rather brightly*) There is just one question I would like to be allowed to ask my guardian.

GWENDOLEN An admirable idea! Mr Worthing, there is just one question I would like to be permitted to put to you. Where is your brother Ernest? We are both engaged to be married to your brother Ernest, so it is a matter of some importance to us to know where your brother Ernest is at present.

JACK (*slowly and hesitatingly*) Gwendolen – Cecily – it is very painful for me to be forced to speak the truth. It is the first time in my life that I have ever been reduced to such a painful position, and I am really quite inexperienced in doing anything of the kind. However, I will tell you quite frankly that I have no brother Ernest. I have no brother at all. I never had a brother in my life, and I certainly have not the smallest intention of ever having one in the future.

CECILY (*surprised*) No brother at all?

JACK (*cheerily*) None!

GWENDOLEN (*severely*) Had you never a brother of any kind?

JACK (*pleasantly*) Never. Not even of any kind.

GWENDOLEN I am afraid it is quite clear, Cecily, that neither of us is engaged to be married to any one.

CECILY It is not a very pleasant position for a young girl suddenly to find herself in. Is it?

GWENDOLEN Let us go into the house. They will hardly venture to come after us there.

CECILY No, men are so cowardly, aren't they?

They retire into the house with scornful looks.

JACK This ghastly state of things is what you call Bunburying, I suppose?

ALGERNON Yes, and a perfectly wonderful Bunbury it is. The most wonderful Bunbury I have ever had in my life.

JACK Well, you've no right whatsoever to Bunbury here.

ALGERNON That is absurd. One has a right to Bunbury anywhere one chooses. Every serious Bunburyist knows that.

JACK Serious Bunburyist! Good heavens!

ALGERNON Well, one must be serious about something, if one wants to have any amusement in life. I happen to be serious about Bunburying. What on earth you are serious about I haven't got the remotest idea. About everything, I should fancy. You have such an absolutely trivial nature.

JACK Well, the only small satisfaction I have in the whole of this wretched business is that your friend Bunbury is quite exploded. You won't be able to run down to the country quite so often as you used to do, dear Algy. And a very good thing too.

ALGERNON Your brother is a little off colour, isn't he, dear Jack? You won't be able to disappear to London quite so frequently as your wicked custom was. And not a bad thing either.

JACK As for your conduct towards Miss Cardew, I must say that your taking in a sweet, simple, innocent girl like that is quite inexcusable. To say nothing of the fact that she is my ward.

ALGERNON I can see no possible defence at all for your deceiving a brilliant, clever, thoroughly experienced young lady like Miss Fairfax. To say nothing of the fact that she is my cousin.

JACK I wanted to be engaged to Gwendolen, that is all. I love her.

ALGERNON Well, I simply wanted to be engaged to Cecily. I adore her.

JACK There is certainly no chance of your marrying Miss Cardew.

ALGERNON I don't think there is much likelihood, Jack, of you and Miss Fairfax being united.

JACK Well, that is no business of yours.

ALGERNON If it was my business, I wouldn't talk about it. (*Begins to eat muffins.*) It is very vulgar to talk about one's business. Only people like stockbrokers do that, and then merely at dinner parties.

JACK How can you sit there, calmly eating muffins when we are in this horrible trouble, I can't make out. You seem to be perfectly heartless.

ALGERNON Well, I can't eat muffins in an agitated manner. The butter would probably get on my cuffs. One should always eat muffins quite calmly. It is the only way to eat them.

JACK I say it's perfectly heartless your eating muffins at all, under the circumstances.

ALGERNON When I am in trouble, eating is the only thing that consoles me. Indeed, when I am in really great trouble, as any one who knows me intimately will tell you, I refuse everything except food and drink. At the present moment I am eating muffins because I am unhappy. Besides, I am particularly fond of muffins. (*Rising.*)

JACK (*rising*) Well, that is no reason why you should eat them all in that greedy way.

51

Takes muffins from Algernon.

ALGERNON (*offering tea-cake*) I wish you would have tea-cake instead. I don't like tea-cake.

JACK Good heavens! I suppose a man may eat his own muffins in his own garden.

ALGERNON But you have just said it was perfectly heartless to eat muffins.

JACK I said it was perfectly heartless of you, under the circumstances. That is a very different thing.

ALGERNON That may be. But the muffins are the same.

He seizes the muffin-dish from Jack.

JACK Algy, I wish to goodness you would go.

ALGERNON You can't possibly ask me to go without having some dinner. It's absurd. I never go without my dinner. No one ever does, except vegetarians and people like that. Besides I have just made arrangements with Dr Chasuble to be christened at a quarter to six under the name of Ernest.

JACK My dear fellow, the sooner you give up that nonsense the better. I made arrangements this morning with Dr Chasuble to be christened myself at 5.30, and I naturally will take the name of Ernest. Gwendolen would wish it. We can't both be christened Ernest. It's absurd. Besides, I have a perfect right to be christened if I like. There is no evidence at all that I have ever been christened by anybody. I should think it extremely probable I never was, and so does Dr Chasuble. It is entirely different in your case. You have been christened already.

ALGERNON Yes, but I have not been christened for years.

JACK Yes, but you have been christened. That is the important thing.

ALGERNON Quite so. So I know my constitution can stand it. If you are not quite sure about your ever having been christened, I must say I think it rather dangerous your venturing on it now. It might make you very unwell. You can hardly have forgotten that some one very closely connected with you was very nearly carried off this week in Paris by a severe chill.

JACK Yes, but you said yourself that a severe chill was not hereditary.

ALGERNON It usen't to be, I know – but I daresay it is now. Science is always making wonderful improvements in things.

JACK (*picking up the muffin-dish*) Oh, that is nonsense; you are always talking nonsense.

ALGERNON Jack, you are at the muffins again! I wish you wouldn't. There are only two left. (*Takes them.*) I told you I was particularly fond of muffins.

JACK But I hate tea-cake.

ALGERNON Why on earth then do you allow tea-cake to be served up for your guests? What ideas you have of hospitality!

JACK Algernon! I have already told you to go. I don't want you here. Why don't you go!

ALGERNON I haven't quite finished my tea yet! and there is still one muffin left.

Jack groans, and sinks into a chair. Algernon still continues eating.

Act Drop

Act Three

Morning-room at the Manor House.

Gwendolen and Cecily are at the window, looking out into the garden.

GWENDOLEN The fact that they did not follow us at once into the house, as any one else would have done, seems to me to show that they have some sense of shame left.

CECILY They have been eating muffins. That looks like repentance.

GWENDOLEN (*after a pause*) They don't seem to notice us at all. Couldn't you cough?

CECILY But I haven't got a cough.

GWENDOLEN They're looking at us. What effrontery!

CECILY They're approaching. That's very forward of them.

GWENDOLEN Let us preserve a dignified silence.

CECILY Certainly. It's the only thing to do now.

Enter Jack followed by Algernon. They whistle some dreadful popular air from a British opera.

GWENDOLEN This dignified silence seems to produce an unpleasant effect.

CECILY A most distasteful one.

GWENDOLEN But we will not be the first to speak.

CECILY Certainly not.

GWENDOLEN Mr Worthing, I have something very particular to ask you. Much depends on your reply.

CECILY Gwendolen, your common sense is invaluable. Mr Moncrieff, kindly answer me the following question. Why did you pretend to be my guardian's brother?

ALGERNON In order that I might have an opportunity of meeting you.

CECILY (*to Gwendolen*) That certainly seems a satisfactory explanation, does it not?

GWENDOLEN Yes, dear, if you can believe him.

CECILY I don't. But that does not affect the wonderful beauty of his answer.

GWENDOLEN True. In matters of grave importance, style, not sincerity is the vital thing. Mr Worthing, what explanation can you offer to me for pretending to have a brother? Was it in order that you might have an opportunity of coming up to town to see me as often as possible?

JACK Can you doubt it, Miss Fairfax?

GWENDOLEN I have the gravest doubts upon the subject. But I intend to crush them. This is not the moment for German scepticism. (*Moving to Cecily.*) Their explanations appear to be quite satisfactory, especially Mr Worthing's. That seems to me to have the stamp of truth upon it.

CECILY I am more than content with what Mr Moncrieff said. His voice alone inspires one with absolute credulity.

GWENDOLEN Then you think we should forgive them?

CECILY Yes. I mean no.

GWENDOLEN True! I had forgotten. There are principles at stake that one cannot surrender. Which of us should tell them? The task is not a pleasant one.

CECILY Could we not both speak at the same time?

GWENDOLEN An excellent idea! I nearly always speak at the same time as other people. Will you take the time from me?

CECILY Certainly.

Gwendolen beats time with uplifted finger.

GWENDOLEN and CECILY (*speaking together*) Your Christian names are still an insuperable barrier. That is all!

JACK and ALGERNON (*speaking together*) Our Christian names! Is that all? But we are going to be christened this afternoon.

GWENDOLEN (*to Jack*) For my sake you are prepared to do this terrible thing?

JACK I am.

CECILY (*to Algernon*) To please me you are ready to face this fearful ordeal?

ALGERNON I am!

GWENDOLEN How absurd to talk of the equality of the sexes! Where questions of self-sacrifice are concerned, men are infinitely beyond us.

JACK We are. (*Clasps hands with Algernon.*)

CECILY They have moments of physical courage of which we women know absolutely nothing.

GWENDOLEN (*to Jack*) Darling!

ALGERNON (*to Cecily*) Darling!

They fall into each other's arms. Enter Merriman. When he enters he coughs loudly, seeing the situation.

MERRIMAN Ahem! Ahem! Lady Bracknell!

JACK Good heavens!

Enter Lady Bracknell. The couples separate in alarm. Exit Merriman.

LADY BRACKNELL Gwendolen! What does this mean?

GWENDOLEN Merely that I am engaged to be married to Mr Worthing, mamma.

LADY BRACKNELL Come here. Sit down. Sit down immediately. Hesitation of any kind is a sign of mental decay in the young, of physical weakness in the old. (*Turns to Jack.*) Apprised, sir, of my daughter's sudden flight by her trusty maid, whose confidence I purchased by means of a small coin, I followed her at once by a luggage train. Her unhappy father is, I am glad to say, under the impression that she is attending a more than usually lengthy lecture by the University Extension Scheme on the Influence of a permanent income on Thought. I do not propose to undeceive him. Indeed I have never undeceived him on any question. I would consider it wrong. But of course, you will clearly understand that all communication between yourself and my daughter must cease immediately from this moment. On this point, as indeed on all points, I am firm.

JACK I am engaged to be married to Gwendolen, Lady Bracknell!

LADY BRACKNELL You are nothing of the kind, sir. And now, as regards Algernon!...Algernon!

ALGERNON Yes, Aunt Augusta.

LADY BRACKNELL May I ask if it is in this house that your invalid friend Mr Bunbury resides?

ALGERNON (*stammering*) Oh! No! Bunbury doesn't live here. Bunbury is somewhere else at present. In fact, Bunbury is dead.

LADY BRACKNELL Dead! When did Mr Bunbury die? His death must have been extremely sudden.

ALGERNON (*airily*) Oh! I killed Bunbury this afternoon. I mean poor Bunbury died this afternoon.

LADY BRACKNELL What did he die of?

ALGERNON Bunbury? Oh, he was quite exploded.

LADY BRACKNELL Exploded! Was he the victim of a revolutionary outrage? I was not aware that Mr Bunbury was interested in social legislation. If so, he is well punished for his morbidity.

ALGERNON My dear Aunt Augusta, I mean he was found out! The doctors found out that Bunbury could not live, that is what I mean – so Bunbury died.

LADY BRACKNELL He seems to have had great confidence in the opinion of his physicians. I am glad, however, that he made up his mind at the last to some definite course of action, and acted under proper medical advice. And now that we have finally got rid of this Mr Bunbury, may I ask, Mr Worthing, who is that young person whose hand my nephew Algernon is now holding in what seems to me a peculiarly unnecessary manner?

JACK That lady is Miss Cecily Cardew, my ward.

Lady Bracknell bows coldly to Cecily.

ALGERNON I am engaged to be married to Cecily, Aunt Augusta.

LADY BRACKNELL I beg your pardon?

CECILY Mr Moncrieff and I are engaged to be married, Lady Bracknell.

LADY BRACKNELL (*with a shiver, crossing to the sofa and sitting down*) I do not know whether there is anything peculiarly exciting in the air of this particular part of Hertfordshire,

but the number of engagements that go on seems to me considerably above the proper average that statistics have laid
down for our guidance. I think some preliminary inquiry on
my part would not be out of place. Mr Worthing, is Miss
Cardew at all connected with any of the larger railway stations in London? I merely desire information. Until yesterday I had no idea that there were any families or persons
whose origin was a Terminus.

Jack looks perfectly furious, but restrains himself.

JACK (*in a clear, cold voice*) Miss Cardew is the grand-daughter
of the late Mr Thomas Cardew of 149 Belgrave Square,
S.W.; Gervase Park, Dorking, Surrey; and the Sporran,
Fifeshire, N.B.

LADY BRACKNELL That sounds not unsatisfactory. Three
addresses always inspire confidence, even in tradesmen. But
what proof have I of their authenticity?

JACK I have carefully preserved the Court Guides of the
period. They are open to your inspection, Lady Bracknell.

LADY BRACKNELL (*grimly*) I have known strange errors in that
publication.

JACK Miss Cardew's family solicitors are Messrs Markby,
Markby, and Markby.

LADY BRACKNELL Markby, Markby, and Markby? A firm of
the very highest position in their profession. Indeed I am
told that one of the Mr Markbys is occasionally to be seen at
dinner parties. So far I am satisfied.

JACK (*very irritably*) How extremely kind of you, Lady Bracknell! I have also in my possession, you will be pleased to
hear, certificates of Miss Cardew's birth, baptism, whooping
cough, registration, vaccination, confirmation, and the
measles; both the German and the English variety.

LADY BRACKNELL Ah! A life crowded with incident, I see;
though perhaps somewhat too exciting for a young girl. I am
not myself in favour of premature experiences! (*Rises, looks at
her watch.*) Gwendolen! the time approaches for our depar-
ture. We have not a moment to lose. As a matter of form,

Mr Worthing, I had better ask you if Miss Cardew has any little fortune?

JACK Oh! about a hundred and thirty thousand pounds in the Funds. That is all. Good-bye, Lady Bracknell. So pleased to have seen you.

LADY BRACKNELL (*sitting down again*) A moment, Mr Worthing. A hundred and thirty thousand pounds! And in the Funds! Miss Cardew seems to me a most attractive young lady, now I look at her. Few girls of the present day have any really solid qualities, any of the qualities that last, and improve with time. We live, I regret to say, in an age of surfaces. (*To Cecily.*) Come over here, dear. (*Cecily goes across.*) Pretty child! your dress is sadly simple, and your hair seems almost as Nature might have left it. But we can soon alter all that. A thoroughly experienced French maid produces a really marvellous result in a very brief space of time. I remember recommending one to young Lady Lancing, and after three months her own husband did not know her.

JACK And after six months nobody knew her.

LADY BRACKNELL (*Glares at Jack for a few moments. Then bends, with a practised smile, to Cecily*) Kindly turn round, sweet child.

Cecily turns completely round.

No, the side view is what I want.

Cecily presents her profile.

Yes, quite as I expected. There are distinct social possibilities in your profile. The two weak points in our age are its want of principle and its want of profile. The chin a little higher, dear. Style largely depends on the way the chin is worn. They are worn very high, just at present. Algernon!

ALGERNON Yes, Aunt Augusta!

LADY BRACKNELL There are distinct social possibilities in Miss Cardew's profile.

ALGERNON Cecily is the sweetest, dearest, prettiest girl in the whole world. And I don't care twopence about social possibilities.

LADY BRACKNELL Never speak disrespectfully of Society, Algernon. Only people who can't get into it do that. (*To Cecily.*) Dear child, of course you know that Algernon has nothing but his debts to depend upon. But I do not approve of mercenary marriages. When I married Lord Bracknell I had no fortune of any kind. But I never dreamed for a moment of allowing that to stand in my way. Well, I suppose I must give my consent.

ALGERNON Thank you, Aunt Augusta.

LADY BRACKNELL Cecily, you may kiss me!

CECILY (*kisses her*) Thank you, Lady Bracknell.

LADY BRACKNELL You may also address me as Aunt Augusta for the future.

CECILY Thank you, Aunt Augusta.

LADY BRACKNELL The marriage, I think, had better take place quite soon.

ALGERNON Thank you, Aunt Augusta.

CECILY Thank you, Aunt Augusta.

LADY BRACKNELL To speak frankly, I am not in favour of long engagements. They give people the opportunity of finding out each other's character before marriage, which I think is never advisable.

JACK I beg pardon for interrupting you, Lady Bracknell, but this engagement is quite out of the question. I am Miss Cardew's guardian, and she cannot marry without my consent until she comes of age. That consent I absolutely decline to give.

LADY BRACKNELL Upon what grounds may I ask? Algernon is an extremely, I may almost say an ostentatiously, eligible young man. He has nothing, but he looks everything. What more can one desire?

JACK It pains me very much to have to speak frankly to you, Lady Bracknell, about your nephew, but the fact is that I do not approve at all of his moral character. I suspect him of being untruthful.

Algernon and Cecily look at him in indignant amazement.

LADY BRACKNELL Untruthful! My nephew Algernon? Impossible! He is an Oxonian.

JACK I fear there can be no possible doubt about the matter. This afternoon during my temporary absence in London on an important question of romance, he obtained admission to my house by means of the false pretence of being my brother. Under an assumed name he drank, I've just been informed by my butler, an entire pint bottle of my Perrier-Jouet, Brut, '89; wine I was specially reserving for myself. Continuing his disgraceful deception, he succeeded in the course of the afternoon in alienating the affections of my only ward. He subsequently stayed to tea, and devoured every single muffin. And what makes his conduct all the more heartless is, that he was perfectly well aware from the first that I have no brother, that I never had a brother, and that I don't intend to have a brother, not even of any kind. I distinctly told him so myself yesterday afternoon.

LADY BRACKNELL Ahem! Mr Worthing, after careful consideration I have decided entirely to overlook my nephew's conduct to you.

JACK That is very generous of you, Lady Bracknell. My own decision, however, is unalterable. I decline to give my consent.

LADY BRACKNELL (*to Cecily*) Come here, sweet child.

Cecily goes over.

How old are you, dear?

CECILY Well, I am really only eighteen, but I always admit to twenty when I go to evening parties.

LADY BRACKNELL You are perfectly right in making some slight alteration. Indeed, no woman should ever be quite accurate about her age. It looks so calculating.... (*In a meditative manner.*) Eighteen, but admitting to twenty at evening parties. Well, it will not be very long before you are of age and free from the restraints of tutelage. So I don't think your guardian's consent is, after all, a matter of any importance.

61

JACK Pray excuse me, Lady Bracknell, for interrupting you again, but it is only fair to tell you that according to the terms of her grandfather's will Miss Cardew does not come legally of age till she is thirty-five.

LADY BRACKNELL That does not seem to me to be a grave objection. Thirty-five is a very attractive age. London society is full of women of the very highest birth who have, of their own free choice, remained thirty-five for years. Lady Dumbleton is an instance in point. To my own knowledge she has been thirty-five ever since she arrived at the age of forty, which was many years ago now. I see no reason why our dear Cecily should not be even still more attractive at the age you mention than she is at present. There will be a large accumulation of property.

CECILY Algy, could you wait for me till I was thirty-five?

ALGERNON Of course I could, Cecily. You know I could.

CECILY Yes, I felt it instinctively, but I couldn't wait all that time. I hate waiting even five minutes for anybody. It always makes me rather cross. I am not punctual myself, I know, but I do like punctuality in others, and waiting, even to be married, is quite out of the question.

ALGERNON Then what is to be done, Cecily?

CECILY I don't know, Mr Moncrieff.

LADY BRACKNELL My dear Mr Worthing, as Miss Cardew states positively that she cannot wait till she is thirty-five – a remark which I am bound to say seems to me to show a somewhat impatient nature – I would beg of you to reconsider your decision.

JACK But my dear Lady Bracknell, the matter is entirely in your own hands. The moment you consent to my marriage with Gwendolen, I will most gladly allow your nephew to form an alliance with my ward.

LADY BRACKNELL (*rising and drawing herself up*) You must be quite aware that what you propose is out of the question.

JACK Then a passionate celibacy is all that any of us can look forward to.

LADY BRACKNELL That is the destiny I propose for Gwendolen. Algernon, of course, can choose for himself. (*Pulls out her watch.*) Come, dear, (*Gwendolen rises*) we have already missed five, if not six, trains. To miss any more might expose us to comment on the platform.

Enter Dr Chasuble.

CHASUBLE Everything is quite ready for the christenings.

LADY BRACKNELL The christenings, sir! Is not that somewhat premature?

CHASUBLE (*looking rather puzzled, and pointing to Jack and Algernon*) Both these gentlemen have expressed a desire for immediate baptism.

LADY BRACKNELL At their age? The idea is grotesque and irreligious! Algernon, I forbid you to be baptized. I will not hear of such excesses. Lord Bracknell would be highly displeased if he learned that that was the way in which you wasted your time and money.

CHASUBLE Am I to understand then that there are to be no christenings at all this afternoon?

JACK I don't think that, as things are now, it would be of much practical value to either of us, Dr Chasuble.

CHASUBLE I am grieved to hear such sentiments from you, Mr Worthing. They savour of the heretical views of the Anabaptists, views that I have completely refuted in four of my unpublished sermons. However, as your present mood seems to be one peculiarly secular, I will return to the church at once. Indeed, I have just been informed by the pew-opener that for the last hour and a half Miss Prism has been waiting for me in the vestry.

LADY BRACKNELL (*starting*) Miss Prism! Did I hear you mention a Miss Prism?

CHASUBLE Yes, Lady Bracknell. I am on my way to join her.

LADY BRACKNELL Pray allow me to detain you for a moment. This matter may prove to be one of vital importance to Lord Bracknell and myself. Is this Miss Prism a female of repellent aspect, remotely connected with education?

CHASUBLE (*somewhat indignantly*) She is the most cultivated of ladies, and the very picture of respectability.

LADY BRACKNELL It is obviously the same person. May I ask what position she holds in your household?

CHASUBLE (*severely*) I am a celibate, madam.

JACK (*interposing*) Miss Prism, Lady Bracknell, has been for the last three years Miss Cardew's esteemed governess and valued companion.

LADY BRACKNELL In spite of what I hear of her, I must see her at once. Let her be sent for.

CHASUBLE (*looking off*) She approaches; she is nigh.

Enter Miss Prism hurriedly.

MISS PRISM I was told you expected me in the vestry, dear Canon. I have been waiting for you there for an hour and three-quarters.

Catches sight of Lady Bracknell, who has fixed her with a stony glare. Miss Prism grows pale and quails. She looks anxiously round as if desirous to escape.

LADY BRACKNELL (*in a severe, judicial voice*) Prism! (*Miss Prism bows her head in shame.*) Come here, Prism! (*Miss Prism approaches in a humble manner.*) Prism! Where is that baby?

General consternation. The Canon starts back in horror. Algernon and Jack pretend to be anxious to shield Cecily and Gwendolen from hearing the details of a terrible public scandal.

Twenty-eight years ago, Prism, you left Lord Bracknell's house, Number 104, Upper Grosvenor Street, in charge of a perambulator that contained a baby of the male sex. You never returned. A few weeks later, through the elaborate investigations of the Metropolitan police, the perambulator was discovered at midnight, standing by itself in a remote corner of Bayswater. It contained the manuscript of a three-volume novel of more than usually revolting sentimentality.

Miss Prism starts in involuntary indignation.

But the baby was not there!

Every one looks at Miss Prism.

Prism! Where is that baby?

A pause.

MISS PRISM Lady Bracknell, I admit with shame that I do not know. I only wish I did. The plain facts of the case are these. On the morning of the day you mention, a day that is for ever branded on my memory, I prepared as usual to take the baby out in its perambulator. I had also with me a somewhat old, but capacious hand-bag in which I had intended to place the manuscript of a work of fiction that I had written during my few unoccupied hours. In a moment of mental abstraction, for which I never can forgive myself, I deposited the manuscript in the basinette, and placed the baby in the hand-bag.

JACK (*who has been listening attentively*) But where did you deposit the hand-bag?

MISS PRISM Do not ask me, Mr Worthing.

JACK Miss Prism, this is a matter of no small importance to me. I insist on knowing where you deposited the hand-bag that contained that infant.

MISS PRISM I left it in the cloakroom of one of the larger railway stations in London.

JACK What railway station?

MISS PRISM (*quite crushed*) Victoria. The Brighton line.

Sinks into a chair.

JACK I must retire to my room for a moment. Gwendolen, wait here for me.

GWENDOLEN If you are not too long, I will wait here for you all my life.

Exit Jack in great excitement.

CHASUBLE What do you think this means, Lady Bracknell?

LADY BRACKNELL I dare not even suspect, Dr Chasuble. I need hardly tell you that in families of high position strange coincidences are not supposed to occur. They are hardly considered the thing.

Noises are heard overhead as if some one was throwing trunks about. Every one looks up.

CECILY Uncle Jack seems strangely agitated.

CHASUBLE Your guardian has a very emotional nature.

LADY BRACKNELL This noise is extremely unpleasant. It sounds as if he was having an argument. I dislike arguments of any kind. They are always vulgar, and often convincing.

CHASUBLE (*looking up*) It has stopped now.

The noise is redoubled.

LADY BRACKNELL I wish he would arrive at some conclusion.

GWENDOLEN This suspense is terrible. I hope it will last.

Enter Jack with a hand-bag of black leather in his hand.

JACK (*rushing over to Miss Prism*) Is this the hand-bag, Miss Prism? Examine it carefully before you speak. The happiness of more than one life depends on your answer.

MISS PRISM (*calmly*) It seems to be mine. Yes, here is the injury it received through the upsetting of a Gower Street omnibus in younger and happier days. Here is the stain on the lining caused by the explosion of a temperance beverage, an incident that occurred at Leamington. And here, on the lock, are my initials. I had forgotten that in an extravagant mood I had had them placed there. The bag is undoubtedly mine. I am delighted to have it so unexpectedly restored to me. It has been a great inconvenience being without it all these years.

JACK (*in a pathetic voice*) Miss Prism, more is restored to you than this hand-bag. I was the baby you placed in it.

MISS PRISM (*amazed*) You?

JACK (*embracing her*). Yes . . . mother!

MISS PRISM (*recoiling in indignant astonishment*) Mr Worthing! I am unmarried!

JACK Unmarried! I do not deny that is a serious blow. But after all, who has the right to cast a stone against one who has suffered? Cannot repentance wipe out an act of folly? Why should there be one law for men, and another for women? Mother, I forgive you.

Tries to embrace her again.

MISS PRISM (*still more indignant*) Mr Worthing, there is some error. (*Pointing to Lady Bracknell.*) There is the lady who can tell you who you really are.

JACK (*after a pause*) Lady Bracknell, I hate to seem inquisitive, but would you kindly inform me who I am?

LADY BRACKNELL I am afraid that the news I have to give you will not altogether please you You are the son of my poor sister, Mrs Moncrieff, and consequently Algernon's elder brother.

JACK Algy's elder brother! Then I have a brother after all. I knew I had a brother! I always said I had a brother! Cecily, – how could you have ever doubted that I had a brother? (*Seizes hold of Algernon.*) Dr Chasuble, my unfortunate brother. Miss Prism, my unfortunate brother. Gwendolen, my unfortunate brother. Algy, you young scoundrel, you will have to treat me with more respect in the future. You have never behaved to me like a brother in all your life.

ALGERNON Well, not till to-day, old boy, I admit. I did my best, however, though I was out of practice.

Shakes hands.

GWENDOLEN (*to Jack*) My own! But what own are you? What is your Christian name, now that you have become some one else?

JACK Good heavens!... I had quite forgotten that point. Your decision on the subject of my name is irrevocable, I suppose?

GWENDOLEN I never change, except in my affections.

CECILY What a noble nature you have, Gwendolen!

JACK Then the question had better be cleared up at once. Aunt Augusta, a moment. At the time when Miss Prism left me in the hand-bag, had I been christened already?

LADY BRACKNELL Every luxury that money could buy, including christening, had been lavished on you by your fond and doting parents.

JACK Then I was christened! That is settled. Now, what name was I given? Let me know the worst.

LADY BRACKNELL Being the eldest son you were naturally christened after your father.

JACK (*irritably*) Yes, but what was my father's Christian name?

LADY BRACKNELL (*meditatively*) I cannot at the present moment recall what the General's Christian name was. But I have no doubt he had one. He was eccentric, I admit. But only in later years. And that was the result of the Indian climate, and marriage, and indigestion, and other things of that kind.

JACK Algy! Can't you recollect what our father's Christian name was?

ALGERNON My dear boy, we were never even on speaking terms. He died before I was a year old.

JACK His name would appear in the Army Lists of the period, I suppose, Aunt Augusta?

LADY BRACKNELL The General was essentially a man of peace, except in his domestic life. But I have no doubt his name would appear in any military directory.

JACK The Army Lists of the last forty years are here. These delightful records should have been my constant study. (*Rushes to bookcase and tears the books out.*) M. Generals... Mallam, Maxbohm, Magley, what ghastly names they have —Markby, Migsby, Mobbs, Moncrieff! Lieutenant 1840, Captain, Lieutenant-Colonel, Colonel, General 1869, Christian names, Ernest John. (*Puts book very quietly down and speaks quite calmly.*) I always told you, Gwendolen, my name was Ernest, didn't I? Well, it is Ernest after all. I mean it naturally is Ernest.

LADY BRACKNELL Yes, I remember now that the General was called Ernest. I knew I had some particular reason for disliking the name.

GWENDOLEN Ernest! My own Ernest! I felt from the first that you could have no other name!

JACK Gwendolen, it is a terrible thing for a man to find out suddenly that all his life he has been speaking nothing but the truth. Can you forgive me?

GWENDOLEN I can. For I feel that you are sure to change.

JACK My own one!

CHASUBLE (*to Miss Prism*) Laetitia!

Embraces her.

MISS PRISM (*enthusiastically*) Frederick! At last!

ALGERNON Cecily! (*Embraces her.*) At last!

JACK Gwendolen! (*Embraces her.*) At last!

LADY BRACKNELL My nephew, you seem to be displaying signs of triviality.

JACK On the contrary, Aunt Augusta, I've now realised for the first time in my life the vital Importance of Being Earnest.

Tableau

Curtain

Glossary: reading the text

The cast

John Worthing, JP   JP means Justice of the Peace, someone who serves as a magistrate on a voluntary part-time basis. A serious and responsible position.

Reverend Canon Chasuble, DD   DD means Doctor of Divinity, the qualifications of the vicar.

Merriman, a butler   a butler is the head servant in a household.

Lane, a manservant   similar to a butler but working for a person (in this case Algernon) rather than a household.

Hon. Gwendolen Fairfax   Hon. is short for Honourable, a title which shows Gwendolen is from the upper classes but has no other significance.

Miss Prism, a governess   a governess was a teacher employed as a private tutor for the children of wealthy families.

Act 1

1 *morning-room*   room used in the morning, usually because of its position in relation to the sun.

forte   strength, ability.

salver   tray, often of silver, used by servants to carry messages and other small items.

your book   record of items that have been purchased or used.

invariably   always.

demoralising   having a bad effect, corrupting.

in consequence of   due to, because of.

2 *languidly*   in a lazy and carefree way.

lax   easy going, not at all strict.

lower orders   lower classes.

sense of moral responsibility   how to behave properly, with a sense of right and wrong.

customary   usual.

good society   by 'good' Algy means a mixture of civilised, fashionable and wealthy. He would consider himself to be part of good society; the lower orders would not be! (see 'Introduction', page xiii).

airily   in a light and carefree manner.

3 *expressly*   specially.

to propose   to offer marriage.

whose memories are so curiously constituted   who have such peculiar memories.

speculating on   theorising about, discussing ideas about.

4 *cigarette case*   metal case for carrying cigarettes, often given as a gift.

smoking room   room reserved for smokers, i.e. men; if Algy's apartment has a morning room, a smoking room and, probably another reception room, it is a very spacious flat.

inscription   special message engraved (i.e. cut into the surface) on something.

5 *ungentlemanly*   not in the manner of a gentleman.

6 *earnest*   serious.

impression   in a dental sense this means a mark produced by the pressure of teeth or gums on some soft material so that the dentist can prepare false teeth of the right shape. In a more general sense it means an effect left in someone's mind, a mark made in their memory.

incomparable   without equal, something so special that nothing else can be compared with it.

7 *guardian*   a person who looks after the interests of someone until they are able to do so on their own. Cecily would be known as Jack's 'ward'.

candidly   honestly.

to adopt a very high moral tone   to give an appearance of being very correct and responsible.

scrapes   difficult situations.

come up to town   it was common for gentlemen to have a house or flat in town (i.e. London or another capital city such as Dublin or Edinburgh, though possibly another fashionable town such as Bath would do) and another larger house in the country. In 'good society' people came up to town for 'the season' (the summer months) in order to see others and be seen by them and to have a good time.

invaluable   extremely valuable, so good that it would be impossible to put a value on it.

8 *Willis's*   fashionable club where gentlemen could eat, drink, read the papers, play cards and so on.

engaged to Aunt Augusta   not to be married to her! Algy has agreed to go to her dinner party.

sent down with   at such dinner parties the guests would meet in a reception room (often on the first floor, especially in town houses) and then be paired off to go down to the dining room for the meal. They would sit next to (and be expected to talk to) the person with whom they were sent down.

washing ones clean linen in public   this is a typical Wilde reversal of the usual saying 'washing one's dirty linen in public', that is, letting outsiders know about domestic problems.

9 *sententiously*   meaningfully; Jack thinks what he is saying is important.

cynical   taking a pessimistic view, looking on the worst side and expecting people to behave badly.

Wagnerian   Wagner was a German composer. The audience would associate him with loudness.

11 *put my table completely out*   it would mean that she would have to re-arrange the seating at her dinner party (see note to page 8).

shilly-shallying   hesitation, not making up one's mind.

arrange music...last reception   it was common for music to be played after the meal at dinner parties. One of the skills taught by governesses would be singing and the playing of a musical instrument – usually a piano.

end of the season   the social season in London (see note to page 7).

12 *expurgations*   things removed or censored.

13 *glibly*   fluently, in a way which sounds convincing.

a metaphysical speculation   an abstract theory, not to do with physical reality.

Jack is a notorious domesticity for John   Jack is a well known informal way of saying John.

14 *semi-recumbent posture*   half lying down position.

indecorous   not good manners.

15 *eligible young men*   men whom she considers are fit to marry Gwendolen.

16 *bloom*   surface glow, as on a fresh fruit.

17 *Liberal Unionist*   branch of the Liberal party at the time which differed from other Liberals in being against Home Rule for Ireland, i.e. in favour of Union with England.

Tories   Conservatives; we would expect Lady Bracknell to be Conservative.

18 *hand-bag*   not the small container for everyday items but something more the size of an overnight case or travelling bag.

immaterial   unimportant.

...French Revolution...   Lady Bracknell is presumably associating the French Revolution with the breakdown of marriage, the family and all civilised values!

indiscretion   something done rashly, usually against society's moral conventions (the established ways of behaving).

19 *right as a trivet*   perfectly right, from the stability of a trivet, or tripod.

Gorgon   mythical monster with snakes instead of hair whose look turned people to stone.

20 *patronising*   treating someone as if they are lower in status or intelligence.

apoplexy   sudden paralysis due to faulty blood supply to the brain, commonly known as a stroke.

21 *capital*   excellent.

22 *incomprehensible*   impossible to understand. The fact that she finds him ex-
    quisitely incomprehensible presumably means that she enjoys not under-
    standing him...

23 *it is to be surmised*   it is to be assumed or thought.

> 1   'The old fashioned respect for the young is fast dying out' (page 22) is
>   the opposite of what we might expect to be said. What would we expect
>   to be said? Find other examples in Act 1 where what is said is the
>   opposite of what we might expect.
>
> 2   Re-read the scene where Jack is proposing to Gwendolen. What opin-
>   ions do you form of her character?
>
> 3   Is Gwendolen afraid of her mother?
>
> 4   What differences are there between Jack and Algy?

Act 2

25 *his gravity of demeanour*   his serious way of behaving.

26 *according to his own brother's admission is irretrievably weak and*
    vacillating   his brother admits he is weak and unsteady beyond hope of
    recovery.

   three volume novels   novels were commonly published in three sections.
    This does not mean that they were longer than modern novels, only that the
    thickness of the paper was much greater than we are used to now.

   Mudie   presumably a bookseller.

27 *Rector*   clergyman who still had the right to collect the Church tithes or taxes.

   canon   title for a clergyman working for a cathedral.

   Chasuble   usually the name of a ceremonial garment worn by a priest – here
    the name of a character who *is* a priest! From the various titles given to
    Chasuble we might wonder whether Wilde was totally clear about their
    meaning. It may be that he wished simply to stress the very serious, re-
    sponsible and upright (and perhaps boring) nature of the character.

inattentive   not paying attention.

I spoke metaphorically   I did not mean what I said literally. To hang on someone's lips literally would be painful for them. To do so metaphorically means to wait with great interest for every word they speak.

Egeria   female adviser.

A classical allusion...   Greek and Roman writers were sometimes called pagan because they preceded Christianity. A classical allusion is a reference to something written by such authors, in this case it is the fact that Egeria was the nymph who instructed Numa Pompilius.

Evensong   traditional evening service in the Anglican church.

28 *Political Economy*   as a subject of study it would now be known as Economics.

gay and debonair   light-hearted and elegant.

30 *Quixotic*   from the character Don Quixote in the novel by Cervantes: ridiculously romantic, even eccentric or odd.

buttonhole   a flower inserted in the button hole in the lapel of a jacket. The actual button hole is missing from most jackets now and the flower worn at weddings etc. has to be pinned into place.

Maréchal Niel   type of rose.

pink rose   the stress here would be on the word *pink*.

31 *misanthrope*   hater of mankind.

womanthrope   hater of women – though the word does not exist; Miss Prism has made it up.

neologism   a new word or phrase; hence: *neologistic* a term used to describe a new word or phrase.

precept as well as the practice   the rule about how to behave as well as what was actually done.

celibacy   an unmarried state adopted for religious reasons.

leads weaker vessels astray   characters who are weak will be tempted by such unmarried men.

horticulturally   to do with gardens.

crape   fabric, usually dyed black for mourning.

32 *garb of woe*   clothing which indicates sadness.

susceptible to   affected by

interment   burial.

some slight allusion to this tragic domestic affliction   a brief mention of this dreadful family misfortune.

33 *immersion*   to be immersed or covered by something; in this case, water at a baptism.

canonical   according to proper Church law.

36 *reconciliation*   a bringing back to friendship.

portmanteaus   large travelling bags.

dog-cart   not, in this case, a cart pulled by dogs, but a cart originally used for carrying sporting dogs.

38 *equanimity*   calmness.

personification   something abstract (or non-human) made human; in this case Algy describes Cecily as being total perfection in person.

41 *Bankruptcy*   the state of a business (and, less often, a person) which had failed because of an inability to pay debts. The *Bankruptcy Court* is the law court where the legal problems resulting from this would be sorted out.

rites and ceremonials of the Church   the formal and defined activities carried out in the Church.

learned   (stress on the second syllable) someone who has a lot of knowledge or learning.

42 *impetuous*   rash or hasty, doing things without thinking.

philanthropic   generous, doing good to others.

forward   not shy or reserved.

43 *Pray sit down*   old fashioned way of saying 'Do please sit down'.

sphere   area of concern or responsibility.

effeminate   unmanly.

short-sighted   the humour of this passage lies in the absurdity of anyone being brought up to be short-sighted (i.e. unable to see distant objects) as if it were something useful or fashionable! There is additional humour in the seriousness with which Gwendolen states this nonsense.

lorgnette   spectacles with a handle attached.

44 *arduous*   difficult, requiring much work.

I am not sure...unmixed delight   a roundabout way of saying 'I am not sure that I am pleased'; in other words 'I'm displeased'.

alluring   attractive.

But even men...charms of others   even good and responsible men can be affected by pretty women.

45 *chronicle*   report.

under some misconception   suffering from a misunderstanding or mistake.

verify   check.

prior claim   first and therefore better claim. Much of the humour here relies on the elaborate language used by the two girls to give a polite surface appearance to their argument.

meditatively   thoughtfully.

46 *reproach*   blame.

Miss Cardew   the girls stop using first names...

allude   refer.

presumtuous   going somewhere without permission, being impolite.

see a spade I call it a spade   saying which means speaking in a down to earth, straightforward way (unlike the way Cecily and Gwendolen have just been talking). Gwendolen scores a point over Cecily by pretending to be so well bred that she has never even seen such a vulgar thing as a spade.

footman   servant.

The presence...chafe   because the servants are there, the girls feel unable to carry on with their argument, which they are anxious to continue.

in the vicinity   near.

parasol   sunshade (like an umbrella).

47 *agricultural depression*   an agricultural depression was an economic problem arising from low prices for agricultural goods. Cecily puns on the word *depression*.

epidemic   illness which spreads rapidly.

elaborate politeness   Gwendolen is polite to Cecily in an exaggerated way which makes it clear that she feels the opposite.

detestable   hateful.

superciliously   arrogantly, in a manner which looks down on others.

grimace   an unpleasant face – often from tasting something unpleasant.

machinations   plotting.

49 *a gross deception has been practised on both of us*   we have been badly deceived.

50 *venture*   dare.

exploded   destroyed, no longer believable.

51 *ward*   see note to page 7 on 'guardian'.

muffins   soft cakes eaten hot, usually with butter.

stockbrokers   someone who buys and sells stocks and shares for clients.

agitated   disturbed, not relaxed.

intimately   closely.

52 *vegetarians*   those who do not eat meat.

I know my constitution can stand it   I know my health is strong enough to put up with it.

---

1   In what way does your impression of Cecily change, or develop, through Act 2? Look at her conversations with Miss Prism, then with Algernon and lastly with Gwendolen.

2   Is the relationship between Algernon and Jack different in this Act?

3   What will be the effect on the audience of seeing Jack enter dressed in mourning clothes? (page 31)

Act 3

54 *repentance*   being sorry.

effrontery   daring, insolence.

air   tune.

55 *German scepticism*   scepticism is an unwillingness to believe anything unless it is clearly proved; some German philosophers were associated with maintaining this standpoint.

credulity   willingness to believe anything.

insuperable barrier   a barrier which cannot be overcome.

56 *apprised*   informed.

whose confidence I purchased   whom I bribed to tell me.

Influence of a permanent income on Thought   a seemingly meaningful topic which on closer examination looks rather absurd. Wilde is poking fun at the sort of lectures given by the University Extension Scheme for those who wish to improve their education. Modern equivalents of the UES might be Adult Education, the Workers Education Association or University Extra-Mural. Departments.

I do not propose to undeceive him   I am not going to tell him the truth.

57 *revolutionary outrage*   an attack by people from a revolutionary group. Bomb attacks by various terrorist groups, especially anarchists, were common in this period.

social legislation   laws affecting society, usually intended to improve the life of ordinary people.

morbidity   unhealthy interest in death.

physicians   doctors.

peculiarly   strangely, especially.

58 *above the proper average that statistics have laid down for our guidance*   the humour here lies in Lady Bracknell assuming the existence of some figures for the number of engagements in any particular area during any one period of time – and the assumption that it would be proper to keep within such statistics.

origin was a Terminus   whose place of birth (or beginning) was an end (or terminus). A railway station at the end of a line was known as a Terminus – and that is where Jack Worthing was found as a baby.

tradesmen   literally those working in trades rather than the professions; the kind of tradesmen to whom Lady Bracknell refers would be those providing services such as grocery deliveries.

authenticity   correctness.

Court Guides   published accounts of addresses and other details of members of the upper classes.

registration   the official register of birth.

vaccination   medical use of vaccine to prevent disease.

confirmation   ceremony accepting a person fully into the church.

premature   before its proper time.

59 *Funds*   secure form of investment at the time.

qualities that last and improve with time   such as money invested in the Funds!

a practised smile   a smile that has been rehearsed in front of a mirror.

social possibilities in your profile   a profile is the way one's face looks from the side. Lady Bracknell thinks Cecily's profile is likely to be fashionable in upper class society. This is almost as absurd as bringing someone up to be short-sighted.

want of   lack of.

60 *Society*   the fashionable section of the community.

mercenary marriages   marriages undertaken in order to make money.

ostentatiously   too obviously, in a way which draws attention.

61 *Oxonian*   someone who has studied at Oxford University.

under an assumed name   using a false name.

alienating the affections   (in this context) gaining the affections (that is, by taking them away – or alienating them – from someone else).

restraints of tutelage   the restrictions of being a ward.

62 *legally of age*   independent, officially 'grown up'.

highest birth   from the upper classes.

remained thirty-five   continued to give their age as thirty-five.

passionate celibacy   an unmarried state full of great feeling – something of a paradox!

63 *grotesque and irreligious*   peculiarly unpleasant and against religion.

grieved...sentiments   upset to hear such opinions.

They savour of...Anabaptists   there is something in them of the unacceptable opinions of the Anabaptists (a sixteenth-century sect believing in a kind of Christian communism).

refuted   disproved.

secular   non-religious.

pew-opener   someone who showed people to their seats in church.

vestry   small room attached to a church.

repellant aspect   unpleasant appearance, ugly.

64 *cultivated*   refined, civilised.

celibate   unmarried through choice or religious vow.

interposing   coming between.

esteemed   respected.

nigh   close by.

quails   flinches, shrinks from.

judicial   like a judge.

consternation   upset, agitation.

perambulator   pram.

manuscript   original version of a piece of writing, usually in handwriting.

involuntary   without thought.

65 *capacious*   large.

a moment of mental abstraction   when my mind was elsewhere, absent mindedly.

bassinet   pram.

agitated   excited.

66 *omnibus* bus.

temperance beverage a non-alcoholic drink.

recoiling moving away.

the right to cast a stone a reference to the New Testament where Jesus says 'He that is without sin among you, let him first cast a stone at her' (St John 8:7) i.e. who is so perfect that they can afford to accuse others of being sinful?

one law for men... society has traditionally accepted that men will have sexual relations outside marriage but criticised women for doing the same; the so-called 'double-standard'.

67 *inquisitive* very curious.

irrevocable impossible to change.

lavished given extravagantly.

doting very loving (implying an excess of affection).

68 *eccentric* unusual, unconventional.

Army Lists the official published records of who was who in the Armed Services.

M. he is searching under the letter M in the list.

---

1 What impression do you get of Miss Prism in Act 3? Take all the evidence into account – the temperance beverage, the three volume novel and so on.

2 What reasons do you think Jack might have for refusing to give permission for Cecily to marry Algernon other than the explanation he gives (page 60)?

3 What difficulty is still unresolved – though no one seems to mind – at the end of the play?

Study programme

Love and marriage

Much of the play is about proposals, engagements and marriage. Lady Bracknell says: 'An engagement should come to a young girl as a surprise, pleasant or unpleasant, as the case may be. It is hardly a matter that she could be allowed to arrange for herself.' Although this is an exaggeration of what went on at the time of the play, it was common for parents to have a much greater influence over their children's choice of husband or wife than is the case in many cultures today.

The stereotype of a proposal involves the young man buying a ring, finding an appropriate circumstance, going down on one knee (perhaps with the ring in hand) and asking the girl if she will marry him. The girl either says yes or no – or that she'll have to think about it. You might enquire of older people that you know whether this actually happened.

1. If this isn't what happens nowadays and if most marriages are not arranged by parents, how *do* most marriages get going? Find our what you can and then write a scene in a play or chapter in a story in which a proposal (or some kind of agreement to get married) takes place.

2. Arranged marriages remain popular in many cultures. Why might this be so? Is there any evidence that arranged marriages are less happy or successful than 'romantic' marriages?

3. What part does love play in *The Importance of Being Earnest*? Write a short essay.

Characters and relationships

1. By the time you reach the end of the play you should be aware of how each of the main characters is related to the others. Make a family tree diagram to show the relationships. Include Thomas Cardew.

2. In a novel of any substance the characters change in some way by the end of the story. Do any of the characters in *The Importance of Being Earnest* change or develop? If yes, who and how? If not, what conclusion do you draw?

3. Write a story which features Lady Bracknell as one of the main characters.

4. Retell in the form of a short story how Jack came to be lost by Miss Prism and later found by Mr Cardew.

5. *Jack Datafile* – as compiled by Lady Bracknell:
   occupation: smoking
   age:
   income:

   Complete the information and add any other items which, though not stated directly, would probably be true.

   Make a similar one for Algernon.

6. The play is full of people saying clever things and untrue things. Who says anything honest in *The Importance of Being Earnest*? Take a representative section of the play, say ten pages, and make a note of any statement which you feel to be a true and honest one. Make sure you note who is the speaker. Having done this, arrange the main characters in the play in order of their honesty.

   This activity will throw up many questions about the nature of truth and honesty, and about which statements are worth recording – is Jack's statement that he prefers standing (page 15), even if considered honest, really worth noting?

⁊ Write a story or sketch in which one of the characters always tells the truth.

⃞8   ALGERNON   *I love scrapes. They are the only things that are never serious.*

Is there anything in the play which is really serious? Who is the most serious person?

⃞9 Do the characters seem to talk nonsense most of the time? Do they seem to say very little which can be taken seriously?

Listen to conversations at school, at home, wherever you can. How much of them deserves to be taken seriously? Which are the subjects that get discussed most seriously – clothes? football? pop groups? Are we any different to Wilde's characters who treat serious things trivially and trivial things seriously?

Diaries and letters

⃞1 A diary is usually reckoned to be a record of actual events – Cecily's is closer to fiction. Write some of her other diary entries – either for the day which takes place on stage or some other time which you will have to imagine.

⃞2 Write the diary entries for Lane and/or Merriman for the events covered in the play. What would have been their feelings about the main characters?

⃞3 Write the diary entries for a week in the life of any of the characters ten years earlier and/or ten years later.

⃞4 Write one of the letters which Algy discovers Cecily wrote from Ernest to herself.

⃞5 Compose a letter which Bunbury might write in order to ask Algernon to come and visit him urgently – or one written by Jack's younger brother which might cause Jack to return to London.

Time and place

1 What would be the main difficulties of staging *The Importance of Being Earnest* as if it were happening in the 1990s?

- What changes would you have to make to the text? (e.g. references to Liberal Unionists, Cecily having a governess...)
- Would the existence of telephones and other modern means of communication make any changes to the play necessary?
- Would you decide to use different props? Would you keep the same settings?

2 Plan your stage set for each Act. How many ways will there be for the actors to get on stage? Work through the text, deciding who will enter by which door/gate etc and which way they will leave. The entrances and exits should be smooth and logical. Which Act has the greatest number of exits and entrances? Which is the most static Act? Does the movement on stage and the number of arrivals and departures affect how dramatic an Act is?

3 What kinds of stories (whether in books or in films) tend to be set in country houses? How realistic are these stories? Carry out some research into country house parties, 'upstairs/downstairs' life and so on. As well as specialist books on the subject, many general histories of the nineteenth and early twentieth century have sections dealing with this subject. Report back to the group or the class.

Stage properties

4 You are in charge of the props for the play. Make a list, Act by Act of:

- those props which are necessary (e.g. muffins, because the dialogue refers to them); and
- those props which you would like to include simply to make the play seem more realistic or effective.

Be precise in your descriptions of the props. For example, don't list 'a plant' – specify a type of plant. There are all sorts of details you may wish to specify: shape, make, colour, size. A large red parasol for Gwendolen will give a different impression compared to a small white one, for instance.

5 You might also be asked to handle the stage furniture. If you are unsure how much a stage can hold, have a look at your school stage. You don't need to measure it accurately; pacing it out from side to side is quite adequate. Then you can decide how many paces a settee would take, and so on. Make a stage plan for each act and indicate where the stage furniture will be positioned. Remember to leave plenty of room for the actors and actresses.

6 Further work of the same kind could be done with costume. How would you dress Algy to distinguish him from Jack, or Cecily from Gwendolen? (Or would you not wish to?)

These activities can be carried out in groups and the group suggestions shared in a general class session.

New scenes

7 What would be the difficulties involved in staging *The Importance of Being Earnest* as a radio play ?

Having considered the question in relation to the play as a whole, take a section of five or six pages and record them, noting where the meaning is less clear to the listener than it would be to someone watching.

8 If you were making a film version, what extra scenes would you put in? If you are able to watch a film version, what scenes were put in? Why? One of the advantages of film is the use of the *close up*. Choose a section of the play and make a note of where you would make use of close up. Would you always want to concentrate on the face of the person speaking? When might you want to emphasise the expression of one of the listeners?

9 *The Importance of Being Earnest* was originally longer: it had four Acts. Write another scene for the play to fit in before, during or after the existing play. You may introduce other characters if you wish.

☐ Use these lines in a scene of your own, either as part of an expanded *Importance of Being Earnest* or as part of a new play of your own:

Ah, the triumph of hope over experience...

You are not, I detect, a slave to fashion.

It is better to be passionately wrong than mildly right!

I was about to laugh but my intellect intervened.

☐ Take five or six lines from *The Importance of Being Earnest* and use them in a scene of your own.

Responding to the critics

☐ How far do you agree with Wilde's own statement that there is no such thing as a moral or immoral book, that books are well written or badly written and that's all there is to it?

☐ How far do you agree with Wilde's description of *The Importance of Being Earnest*: 'The first act is ingenious, the second beautiful and the third abominably clever'?

☐ Are wit and wordplay the decoration or the substance of *The Importance of Being Earnest*?

☐ 'Loosely concerned with John Worthing's search for his own identify...it is in reality a series of brilliant confidence tricks played by the characters on each other and their audience.' How adequate is this as a description of *The Importance of Being Earnest*?

☐ 'Humour, like drama, arises from conflict.' How far is this true in *The Importance of Being Earnest*?

☐ Is Wilde more interested in *dialogue* than in *character*, as the critic C J L Price suggests?

7 Would you support CJL Price's or Eric Bentley's reaction to the play as expressed on page xiv of the 'Introduction'?

8 How far is the historical setting of the play and the social class of the characters essential to its success?

Beyond the text

Fashion

1 The central characters in the play are very concerned with what is fashionable. For example, Lady Bracknell comments on the fashionable side of Belgrave Square. Gwendolen remarks that 'Cake is rarely seen at the best houses nowadays.' Such remarks seem absurd, yet we are as conscious of fashion now as Gwendolen and Lady Bracknell were then. Clothes are an obvious example – but what other items can become fashionable or unfashionable? Food – cars – ways of decorating your house – types of leisure activity...

Make two lists, one of the things which fashion seems to have an effect on and another one of things on which it seems to have very little effect.

2 Are fashionable things always the most expensive? Are different things fashionable to different types of people? Does being fashionable matter more to some people than others? Can anyone in the class honestly say, 'I don't let fashion affect what I do. I make my own mind up.'? Is it possible to ignore fashion? Answer these questions by considering them yourself and by asking others, including people of different ages and backgrounds.

3 A lot of money is made by businesses which rely on changing fashions to sell new things. What sense would a person from another planet – or even from a third world country – make of throwing out perfectly good clothes simply because they are out of fashion?

4 Collect your conclusions from all these questions and arrange them as logically as possible in an article titled 'Who Cares about Fashion?' for a

magazine aimed at people of your own age or slightly older. Make sure you consider lots of other things besides clothes.

Class and money

5 The central characters in the play are what would be termed Upper Class. What's happened to the upper classes? Do they still exist? Why are they not as powerful as they were in Wilde's day?

Are there people like Jack and Algy nowadays? What would today's equivalents be like?

6 Read (or watch on video) some of P G Wodehouse's stories about Jeeves and Wooster. What similarities are there between the characters in those stories and the people in the play?

7 We all have an image of what it is to be Upper Class, to be a 'Lady' or a 'Gentleman'. What are the qualities which make someone a Lady or a Gentleman? It is merely the possession of lots of money – or not having to work for a living?

8 Bernard Shaw wrote a play called *Pygmalion* which centres on a bet made by Professor Higgins that he can turn a lower class flower seller into a Society lady by changing the way she speaks. He succeeds. How important is it to speak with the 'right' accent?

9 Having considered some of the questions above, write a story or short play in which someone who is not Upper Class pretends to be a Gentleman or Lady or vice versa. Think out the motives for the pretence first, then consider the plot and the characters. Try to concentrate, in your writing, on the problems that the character might have in convincing others. Does he or she succeed?

Situation comedy

10 Look at copies of newspaper TV pages or use the *Radio* and *TV Times* to work out how many comedy programmes there are on each channel.

Which channel broadcasts the most hours of comedy? What different kinds of TV comedy programmes are there? Situation comedy (or 'sit-com') is one kind.

How much comedy is broadcast on radio? On which stations? Does radio concentrate on the same kind of comedy as TV? How would you classify a programme like *Just a Minute*?

▨ Watch three or four different 'sit-com' programmes on television. If you can use a video to stop the programme when you want, that would be an advantage. One common means of getting laughter, from Shakespeare through to ITV, is the witty insult. What other ways are there? Jot down the sort of things that make people laugh — or are intended to make people laugh. This is quite hard to do — but quite enjoyable.

Share your conclusions with the rest of the class. How far can you agree — not about which programmes are funny — but about the sort of things that make people laugh?

▨ *The Importance of Being Earnest* is a situation comedy. Does it make people laugh in the same way as the programmes you have looked at? (There are some interesting omissions in *The Importance of Being Earnest*. Unlike both Shakespeare and ITV, it makes no use of jokes based on sexual double-meanings. See what other differences you can find.)

Names

▨ What's in a name? Ernest... Rose... June...

What other names also have meanings? e.g. Felicity/Felix means happiness. Do you know what your name means? Find out the meaning of the names in your family, including as many relations as you can. What do you think of your own name? What would you like to be called? Why?

▨ Carry out a survey of the most common names in your year at school or college. Compare it with a survey of the most popular names — i.e. people's favourite names.

▣ Some names come and go in popularity. Others always seem popular. Still others are popular only once. Try to find examples of all three categories. What methods could you use to find this information: Collecting names from gravestones? Novels? Family history? Consult a history teacher if in doubt.

Display your findings in a clear and attractive way.

Suggestions for further reading

The Penguin *Collected Plays of Oscar Wilde* includes *A Woman of No Importance*, *Lady Windemere's Fan* and *An Ideal Husband*, all of which make excellent comparisons with *The Importance of Being Earnest*. *Salome*, the other play which is included, is very different! It isn't to everybody's taste, but if you do find it fascinating, it is worth listening to Richard Strauss's opera version which uses Wilde's words.

Also of interest are Wilde's children's stories, especially *The Selfish Giant* and *The Happy Prince*. Both are still widely available, as is Wilde's novel, *The Picture of Dorian Gray*.

Of the many biographies, Sheridan Morley's *Oscar Wilde* is one of the most readable and balanced accounts for the writer's life.

Other plays which deal with similar concerns, e.g. *Pygmalion* by Shaw, *The Rivals* by Sheridan and *She Stoops to Conquer* by Goldsmith make useful comparisons. The farces of Feydeau or the modern comedies of Alan Ayckbourn would provide interesting contrasts – as would the novels of PG Wodehouse, especially those featuring Wooster and his manservant, Jeeves.

There are at least two films of *The Importance of Being Earnest*, which are fairly readily available. There have been a number of films about Oscar Wilde but these are more difficult to obtain. Most record lending libraries of any size will have a recording of the play.

Wider reading assignments

☐ What similarities to *The Importance of Being Earnest* do you notice in *A Woman of No Importance*, *Lady Windemere's Fan* or *An Ideal Husband*? If you are able to compare it with all three, explain why you think *The Importance of Being Earnest* has been the most popular.

☐ Which plays by other writers can you discover which tackle the issue of gaining a marriage partner? Do they have anything in common with Wilde's play(s)? Are such plays likely to be serious or comic? (Why do you think so many of the plays and films which use this theme are comedies? What's funny about getting married?)

☐ Compare Wilde's treatment of love and marriage with Shakespeare's treatment of the same themes in *Twelfth Night*, *The Taming of the Shrew*, *Love's Labours Lost*, *A Midsummer Night's Dream* or *Much Ado About Nothing*. If you haven't the time to read or the opportunity to see the full play(s), a sensibly abridged version would provide an idea of the plots, characters and relationships.

☐ Judging by the stories or plays you have read, is it true that 'The path of true love never did run smooth'? Or is it just that a smooth path doesn't make an interesting story?

Addison Wesley Longman Limited
Edinburgh Gate, Harlow,
Essex CM20 2JE, England

This edition first published 1991
Tenth impression 1997

Editorial Material set in 10/12 pt Helvetica Light Condensed
Produced by Longman Singapore Publishers (Pte) Ltd
Printed in Singapore

The publisher's policy is to use paper manufactured from sustainable forests.

ISBN 0 582 07784 2